Thinking in a Digital World

Thinking in a Digital World

Taking Our Kids into the Deep End

Patricia Calton Buoncristiani
and
Martin Buoncristiani

ROWMAN & LITTLEFIELD
Lanham • Boulder • New York • London

Published by Rowman & Littlefield
A wholly owned subsidiary of The Rowman & Littlefield Publishing Group, Inc.
4501 Forbes Boulevard, Suite 200, Lanham, Maryland 20706
www.rowman.com

Unit A, Whitacre Mews, 26-34 Stannary Street, London SE11 4AB

Copyright © 2017 by Patricia Calton Buoncristiani and Martin Buoncristiani

All rights reserved. No part of this book may be reproduced in any form or by any electronic or mechanical means, including information storage and retrieval systems, without written permission from the publisher, except by a reviewer who may quote passages in a review.

British Library Cataloguing in Publication Information Available

Library of Congress Cataloging-in-Publication Data Available

ISBN: 978-1-4758-3493-2 (cloth : alk. paper)
ISBN: 978-1-4758-3494-9 (pbk. : alk. paper)
ISBN: 978-1-4758-3495-6 (electronic)

♾™ The paper used in this publication meets the minimum requirements of American National Standard for Information Sciences—Permanence of Paper for Printed Library Materials, ANSI/NISO Z39.48-1992.

Printed in the United States of America

We dedicate this book to Dr Arthur Costa who introduced us to the power of deep thinking and has been an unfailing mentor throughout our journey.

When you venture into deep water I want to be sure there is an adult by your side who knows how to keep you safe until you are able to take care of yourself.

You will need to understand the dangers, to anticipate the power of the water and the waves. I want you to learn how to float safely first, and then to swim with confidence and strength. Above all, I want you to feel joy in the experience, to take delight in the waves and the light glinting on the surface and then to explore the depths, the sea floor and everything you can discover there.

The title of this book acknowledges the influence on our thinking of Nicholas Carr's book *The Shallows: What the Internet Is Doing to Our Brains*.

Contents

Foreword by Professor Arthur Costa ... ix

Preface ... xi

Introduction ... xiii

1. Grown-Ups—We Have a Problem: Our Kids Are Trapped in the Shallows ... 1
2. The World Is Changing: From Lines to Webs ... 11
3. Surveying the Landscape: Education and Learning ... 27
4. The Twenty-First Century Needs Us ... 43
5. What Is Happening in Our Schools? ... 49
6. The Digital Divides: Immigrants and Natives, Real and Virtual ... 59
7. Contrary to Popular Opinion, Television Can Help Bridge the Divide ... 69
8. Living in Two Worlds: Tangible and Virtual ... 75
9. The Best of Both Worlds ... 89
10. Safe Enough to Think: Keeping Children Safe and Ensuring Safety of Information ... 95
11. It's Hard to Manage What You Don't Understand ... 107

12	Metacognition: What We Do When We Think in the Deep End	131
13	Behaving Like a Deep-Water Thinker	159
14	Am I Clever Enough to Think in The Deep End?	175
	Conclusion	185
	Bibliography	187
	Index	191

Foreword

I met with a group of parents recently in an elementary school near Boulder, Colorado. Their chief concern was what to do about their children's obsession with their cell phones rather than their homework. Their children come home from school, get a snack, go to their room, engage in social networking, and don't emerge again (with much prodding) until dinnertime.

Having grown up in a different era, many parents are concerned and baffled by what to do about the increase in technological resources available today and what they remembered as appropriate behavior when they were growing up in their homes as a previous generation. The dilemma is that we realize that technology is a valuable resource. Many parents rely on technology in their work or careers. However, their kids become addicted to it. Furthermore, parents expect to have some home life interacting with, enjoying, influencing, and being part of their children's lives.

Patricia and Martin Buoncristiani provide a valuable resource to parents and teachers, helping them to find a balance between the digital world and the physical world, understanding that in both we find value and importance. We do not want to find ourselves with our children on one side of the divide and the teachers and parents on the other side, neither able to comfortably jump the gap.

Children learn how to adapt and regulate their behavior in a variety of life situations. Parents teach their children various forms of etiquette, such as how to behave and talk during dinner with grandparents, what is proper conduct at church or when camping in the wild and how to take a date to the prom. Likewise, teachers teach students proper behavior in class, on the playground, and in the cafeteria. Parents and teachers also need to teach children a kind of digital etiquette ("Netiquette") when using the Internet and social networks.

This includes proper, safe communication of words, thoughts, music, or photographs.

While the Internet is rich in information, it is also filled with undesirable and inaccurate content. One recent study cited claims that 82 percent of middle schoolers couldn't distinguish between an advertisement labeled "sponsored content" and a real news story (Shellenbarger, 2016). Some teens absorb social media news without considering its validity and the source. The authors suggest that children, therefore, need to learn how to think—deeply.

This means that parents and teachers must teach critical thinking, research skills, and skepticism. They must give their youngsters the reasoning tools to analyze and discriminate between that which is valid and that which is undesirable. It means that children need to think about their own thinking (metacognition)—to become self-aware of the circumstances they are in, what kind of thinking and behavior is appropriate, and they must be able to modify their own behaviors accordingly. In other words, to self-manage, self-monitor, and self-modify.

The authors provide rich examples, vignettes and scenarios, and directions for how to talk with children about their thinking and how to pose questions to elicit thoughtful responses and self-examination. Through these examples, children will come to see that sound thinking is valued and that we all benefit when our thinking is deepened. We realize that the technology itself is not inherently dangerous. The danger comes from how we use it.

Arthur L. Costa, EdD
Emeritus Professor of Education at California State University, Sacramento, Co-Founder of the Institute for Habits of Mind and Co-founder of the Center for Cognitive Coaching.

REFERENCE

Shellenbarger, S. (Nov. 21, 2016). Most Students Don't Know When News Is Fake, Stanford Study Finds. New York: The Wall Street Journal.

Preface

The world has changed and continues to change at an ever-increasing rate. Our children's brains are changing too. We have learned that brain architecture is not fixed at birth. It is molded by the experiences we encounter throughout our lives.

The networked, digital world our children are developing in is having a significant effect on how they think.

We will demonstrate the nature of these changes and explain why it is important that the grown-ups understand how young people are interacting with this digital environment.

Our youngsters run the risk of becoming superficial thinkers—knowing a little bit about a great many things, having only a surface understanding about how society works and losing the ability to think in depth and with focus. Their brains are becoming a tangle of impressions, information, emotions, and more.

We provide illustrative examples drawn from our combined forty or more years' experience as educators. We offer practical suggestions and strategies that you can use in the classroom today and ideas that you can share with the parents of the children you teach.

As you read this book we ask you to do some deep thinking. Our intention is to help you understand what is happening so that you will be in a position to design appropriate lessons and interact with students and with your own children in ways that help them become deep thinkers in a digital age.

There are no scripted lessons here, no opportunities to simply choose a strategy and apply it in the classroom on Monday morning. There are plenty of examples drawn from our own experiences both as educators and as parents.

Our intention is not to provide you with easy answers to your youngster's digital experiences.

Instead, we will provide you with the understanding you will need to design strategies that are tailored to *your* circumstances, *your* youngsters, *your* place, and *your* time.

Introduction

In 2015 and 2016, a ten-year study began in Alberta, Canada. Two thousand two hundred seventy-two educators across more than a thousand schools were asked questions about the impact of digital technologies in their lives and in the lives of their students.

While 71 percent of these educators agreed that digital technologies enhanced teaching and learning, their responses to the survey acts as a warning. Sixty-seven percent of teachers stated that digital technologies were distracting their students negatively and more than half of them identified technology as a significant distraction in their own lives. Around 66 percent said that their students' ability to focus had declined, with one teacher saying, "I believe children are becoming passive learners; they don't know how to think on their own." This work was done by Dr Phil McRae, executive staff with the Alberta Teachers' Association and two researchers from the University of Alberta, Drs Stanley Varnhagen and Jason Daniels and Dr Michael Rich of the Harvard Medical School (GUD, 2016).

This is a critical time; we are at risk of creating a generation of shallow, "gist" thinkers. It's time the grown-ups took charge in this digital age.

The teaching of thinking is too important to be left to chance. In every lesson, with every young person's interaction with the digital, online world we must seek to develop deeper thinking. It's about intention. We can be a powerful influence for good if phrases like, "Let's stop for a moment and think about this" are a natural part of our conversations with children.

The 2016 National Education Technology Plan: Future Ready Learning: Reimagining the Role of Technology in Learning (NETP, 2016) makes the following observations:

- *Few schools have adopted approaches for using technology to support informal learning experiences aligned with formal learning goals.*
- *Supporting learners in using technology for out-of-school learning experiences is often a missed opportunity.*
- *Across the board, teacher preparation and professional development programs fail to prepare teachers to use technology in effective ways (p 5).*

We will help you to understand why after so many years of the Internet and digital technology some of us still struggle to use it effectively. We will provide you with a wide range of ideas and strategies to ensure that your students are using digital technology in order to further their ability to think deeply and effectively as they learn.

In this book we explore how the world, the notion of education, and the ways in which our children think are changing. You will also understand what you need to do about it.

- Chapter 1 points to the serious problem educators and parents are facing in this sometimes frenetic and shape-shifting modern, digital world.
- In chapter 2 we examine the shift in focus from linear thinking to dynamic interconnected thinking brought about by the digital age.
- Chapter 3 explores how our understandings of "learning" and "education" have become more complex and interwoven over time.
- Chapter 4 looks at the skills needed to thrive in the twenty-first century.
- Chapter 5 considers the extent to which our school systems have frequently failed to adapt to these growing understandings.
- Chapter 6 examines the digital divide that is developing as a result of these newly predominant ways of thinking and explores ways in which adults can bridge that divide and encourage our youngsters to think more deeply.
- Chapter 7 examines one medium and how it might be used to bridge the divide.
- In chapter 8 we explore the differences between the virtual and the physical worlds and how important it is not to allow the digital world to crowd out the physical world. We consider the different properties of the tangible, physically experiential world and the virtual world and we show the importance of timely disengagement and disentanglement from that virtual world.

- Chapter 9 addresses the argument that we benefit from integrating the virtual and the tangible by considering keyboarding and hand writing.
- Chapter 10 looks closely at safety. You will understand the importance of thinking in depth about the electronic media our youngsters use and how to keep them safe in that challenging territory. We also examine ways to ensure that the information encountered within digital media are reliable. What can we safely believe?
- Chapter 11 explores ways of becoming more familiar and confident with digital media.
- In chapter 12 we explore the nitty gritty of deep water thinking—thinking about our thinking—metacognition.
- Chapter 13 describes some of the behaviors that support deep water thinking. In particular we look at some of the Habits of Mind that will make it possible for our youngsters to think deeply, flexibly, and creatively and to understand their own thought processes. We provide practical strategies that grow out of the CCSS and explore the power of good questioning.
- Finally, in chapter 14 we show that everyone has the capacity to think more deeply and that this capacity persists throughout life. Understanding that the brain is a plastic organ that changes with every experience, every thought, we look at the work of Carol Dweck (Dweck, 2006) and the significance of having a fixed or a growth mindset. This chapter explores the brain's plasticity and the importance of mindset.
- Finally, we offer a list of books for further reading.

Chapter One

Grown-Ups—We Have a Problem
Our Kids Are Trapped in the Shallows

Teachers and parents read books, scour blogs and online resources, attend professional development sessions, and talk with their colleagues, all in an effort to find ways to help kids ENGAGE with the educational process. Engagement has become a buzz word. It may seem surprising, then, that we have written this book in order to demonstrate how important it is to teach youngsters how to DISengage and escape from the entanglement of too much information and not enough understanding.

If you have ever been to Hawaii you may have had the good fortune to swim in the warm waters of Hanauma Bay. With a mask and snorkel you can explore the shallow waters inside the reef and see a myriad brilliant-colored tropical fish swimming fearlessly around you. Their colors are mesmerizing. It's exciting and exhilarating. You will learn a lot about the variety and profusion of sea life.

But if you have the skills of a fairly strong swimmer you can venture beyond the coral reef and into the deeper waters. As you glide from the shallow water across the reef you will see the ocean floor drop precipitately below you. This is a profoundly different experience. It is awe inspiring. There is a sense of calm here, the water is not so busy, and this is where the big fish dwell. In this deep water you are not distracted by the darting little attention seekers inside the reef. Here you can watch the behavior of a single fish as it interacts with the currents, seeks out food, and deals with other fish it might encounter. You can come to a deeper understanding of that fish within its environment. This water may not be as exciting, but it is inspirational.

There is a serious problem facing our young people today. Their digital world is like an ocean, with its shallow ends filled with multimedia light, sight, and movement. They are awash with information, and it's like a profusion of small fishes darting about around them. Attention snaps from one fascination point to another and what they gain is an impression of how amazing the world is.

We want our young people to have the skills they need to move safely out of these shallow waters of the digital world and into the deep water of concentrated, focused, effective thinking. We don't want to deny them the excitement or the value of staying close to the shore and all there is to offer there, but we want them to be able to disengage, to leave the shallows behind from time to time. We want them to develop the habits of deep thinking while being safe and confident in the deep end of the ocean.

Our young people are in serious danger of finding themselves trapped in the shallows. In part, this is because the shallows are so inviting and so fascinating, in part it is because they simply haven't had the opportunity to experience the deeper satisfactions of the deep water. Just as it is our responsibility to ensure our children are safe in the waters they swim in, it is up to us, the adults, to help them develop the skills they need to think deeply and effectively in the world they inhabit.

We need to teach them how to dive deeply below the surface.

IT IS TIME THE GROWN-UPS JUMPED IN THE WATER TOO

To understand how this problem has arisen we need to know something about the history of our understandings about learning and about education. Our beliefs about learning began with a simple thread—tell them, get them to repeat it, then they will know it. Over decades we have learned much about children and about how their brains develop. Sadly the increasing sophistication of our understandings about learning has not translated into the practices of many of our educational institutions.

Our knowledge about how people learn is embedded in a world that has also changed dramatically since the invention of the digital computer and the Internet. Learning is a complex process in a complex world, and both are changing, even as we think about them. Is it any wonder that we sometimes feel "all at sea" as we confront one new learning theory after another? Like brilliant fish, new ideas dart at us, and just when we think we have grasped the latest one it slips from our fingers and another one flashes into view.

Trying to keep up with it all can leave us tearing our hair out as we try to accommodate to block scheduling, brain-based teaching, left brain/right brain, constructivism, cooperative learning, critical thinking, core knowledge, creative thinking, cultural literacy, didactic teaching, emotional intelligence, inquiry-based learning, integrated curriculum, multiple intelligences, Socratic questioning, mindfulness, fixed and growth mind set, character education, discovery learning, thinking hats, habits of mind, competency-based learning, flipped classrooms, whole language literacy learning, phonics-based learning, phonemic awareness—and the list could go on.

We must value the shallows, with all its color and movement. We must also know how to head for deeper water. As the teachers of the next generation it is important for us to be able to filter what is, at times, an overwhelming amount of information, and focus on what is most important and then come to understand it in depth. Sometimes we need to turn away from the little fish and focus on the big ones.

Educators must understand how people learn, how the digital world is changing how people think, and how they can help our youngsters to retain all that is helpful in the digital world without losing the ability to disengage, disentangle, focus, and think in depth.

Building on this understanding we provide you with practical strategies to teach children to be deep thinkers in a digital world. These strategies encompass the classroom and link clearly with the Common Core State Standards (CCSS), as well as ways in which schools can use their home school partnerships to further the thoughtful use of the Internet.

Many teachers are parents and all parents are teachers. Grandparents, aunts and uncles, shopkeepers, police, doctors, librarians, and checkout personnel are teachers too. The National Network of Partnership Schools was established in 1996 at Johns Hopkins University. Extensive research over several decades has demonstrated that when parents, teachers, and communities collaborate in the education of our young people we can assure greater success in their education.

This is a book for anyone who spends time interacting with children and young people, and who takes seriously their role as a mentor, a guide, and being the grown-up. It is primarily a book for teachers and schools, with the understanding that schools are one of the most effective conduits for informing parents and community members about the ways in which they can become involved in the education of the community's children.

As you read and discuss this book you will find opportunities to include the entire school community—parents, grandparents, aunts and uncles, day-care providers, bus drivers, preschool teachers, and anyone you believe has the opportunity to contribute to the growing understanding of the world that you engage with every day as you teach our children.

Chapter One

OUR CHILDREN MUST BE PROBLEM-SOLVERS

The ancient Chinese curse "may you live in interesting times" cannot be far from our minds as we attempt to make sense of the shape-shifting environment in which we live. Our children today are now connected and involved with one another and with the world through their electronic devices in ways anyone born before 1990 can hardly understand.

We repeatedly hear that our children will face a tomorrow that we cannot predict, a world with problems and solutions that will be as novel, mystifying, and exciting as the Internet itself would have been to our grandparents.

It seems only a handful of years ago that we were sitting together quietly one evening. Martin was working with his computer and clearly having some problems. He exclaimed "I think my mouse must be dirty" and we both burst out laughing trying to imagine what our mothers and fathers would have made of this stated dilemma.

The discomforting thought is that our children today don't know what a mouse is in this context. As it was for our parents, a mouse to them is a small, furry rodent that squeaks and gets into the pantry during the winter months. Theirs is a world of touch screens and is becoming one of gestures, as they interact with kinetic game machines that respond to their own physical movements, without them ever having to physically touch anything. A mouse? How terribly last century.

Our parents could not have imagined the things we take for granted today. Anyone over forty can probably think back to their early twenties and have a sense of the enormity of change that this burgeoning electronic age has given us. This speed and scope of change raises a profound question for anyone concerned with the generation of children and young people who will soon be in charge of the world.

If we cannot get our imaginations around what the world will look like in ten or fifteen years how can we help prepare our children to be effective agents within it? To thrive they will need to be able to think effectively, flexibly and creatively.

Over the years we have asked different groups with whom we have worked the same question, "What would you hope your children would have retained five years after they leave school?" The responses have been both fascinating and illuminating, both for their content and for their uniformity.

Everyone seems to feel much the same way, parents, teachers, administrators, employers, seniors groups, and they all tell the same story. They want our children to have appropriate levels of literacy and numeracy, be able to work collaboratively, to be self-sustaining, to be flexible in their thinking, to know how to solve problems, and to be independent life-long learners. No one has mentioned the need to know the dates of first settlement, the signatories to the Treaty of Versailles, or the stages of cell division. No one has mentioned any particular "stuff" as essential for children to learn. Instead the clear focus has been on the development of the behaviors and skills that will enable our young people to be effective participants in any environment, no matter how dynamic or different it may be from what surrounds them now.

No one questions the importance of our young people learning how to think skillfully. The human capacity to think skillfully and in depth is what sets us apart from every other creature on earth. It is our ability to think creatively that has taken us from the cave to the city, from squatting in the forest to having sewerage treatment works, and from dipping a hollow gourd in a river to turning on a tap. It is our delight in solving problems collaboratively that has ensured relief from toothache, the almost total eradication of small pox and polio, and the ability to use the bountiful energy of the sun to heat our homes in winter, keep our ice cream frozen in the summer, and to entertain us in the evening.

WE HAVE BEEN GOOD AT SOLVING PROBLEMS

The history of the human race has been one of problem-solving. London in 1900 used horses to transport people and goods around the ever-growing city—around 50,000 of them altogether. Each horse produced between 5 and 15 kilograms of manure a day. A writer in the *London Times* lamented that within fifty years every London street would be buried under more than 9 feet of manure—that's 2.75 meters. The problem seemed insoluble. But the Great Horse Manure Crisis of the late nineteenth century never happened. Building on the research of others going back as far as the seventeenth century, Karl Benz patented the first practical motor car engine in 1879 and by 1920 a T model Ford was coming off the assembly line every fifteen minutes. It was the efficacy of people's thinking that brought about the age of the motor car.

The Great Horse Manure Crisis was averted by innovation, the capacity of thinkers to bring different ideas together and to think collaboratively across time and space, to learn from and with each other. So it has been time and time again in the past, and so it will be in the future.

Today we face massive challenges to our ingenuity far greater than an excess of horse manure. Climate change, the rapid economic expansion of previously underdeveloped nations, the growing disparity between the rich and the poor and the decline of the middle class, the need to find replacements for finite and perhaps damaging carbon-based energy sources, as well as never-ending geopolitical conflicts, all tell us that the future belongs to the thinkers and to the doers.

We need problem-solvers. Thinking alone will not achieve anything, but action without effective thought will only get us deeper into trouble. We can find enough examples of "shooting from the hip," acting first and thinking later, to know this from bitter experience.

Every advanced society seems to be engaged in some form of educational reform. In the United Kingdom a new curriculum for children between the ages of six and eleven was introduced in 2014. By the end of 2015, older students were also faced with a new curriculum. The curriculum focuses on the knowledge that is deemed necessary for children to obtain during their schooling. It doesn't tell teachers how to teach this knowledge, leaving it up to educators in the schools to shape learning activities to suit their populations.

Similar moves are taking place in Australia with the implementation of a national curriculum. It is expected that every child in Australia will be taught the same content regardless of where they live geographically and regardless of their background. Here, too, teachers are not told how to teach, only what to teach.

In 2009 in the United States, leaders in education from forty-eight states together developed the Common Core, a set of clear college- and career-ready standards covering kindergarten to year 12 in the curriculum areas of English language arts/literacy and mathematics. The following year the States developed their own The CCSS based on these original standards. Although the adoption of these standards was voluntary, by 2013, forty-two states had come on board.

TECHNOLOGY IN THE CCSS

Every new curriculum has attempted to integrate digital technology as learning tools. The CCSS makes reference to "technology" in almost every learning goal and expects students to become "strategic" users of digital technology. What these standards fail to do in any detail is acknowledge the extent to which these digital technologies are changing how we think, how we do things, and how we relate to one another.

In the *English Language Arts Standards: Introduction: How to Read the Standards* we read:

> the Speaking and Listening standards require students to develop a range of broadly useful oral communication and interpersonal skills. Students must learn to work together, express and listen carefully to ideas, integrate information from oral, visual, quantitative, and media sources, evaluate what they hear, use

media and visual displays strategically to help achieve communicative purposes, and adapt speech to context and task.

It is impossible to fulfill the goals of working together, communicating effectively, and integrating what we learn into our lives without also addressing the issues we explore in this book.

The digital age is changing the way our children think. The world of the Internet is a rich source of learning and a powerful tool for collaboration. If we grown-ups fail to understand it and how it impacts our youngsters, if we try and pretend it isn't there, or attempt to work our way around it rather than encompassing it, we are in danger of losing the baby with the bath water.

Whether within the school or outside the classroom walls, it is imperative that we recognize the forces that are encouraging our young people to think superficially about a vast number of things, rather than thinking in depth about a few.

DIVING DEEPER, SLOWING DOWN, AND KEEPING STILL

Every good teacher knows that the use of nonlinguistic representations and analogies can help our understanding.

Let's get back in the ocean. Wearing a mask and snorkel look around you. Isn't it all amazing? The fractured, flashing light as it filters through the water, the feet of other bathers as they splash about in the shallows, the swirling sand as feet kick it up and water carries it along. There are shells of so many shapes, sizes, and colors, swathes of seaweed, and shoals of tiny fish darting past you. They flash into the distance while a new shoal appears just beyond the limits of your vision. You can feel the rush of water, the sudden temperature changes, and the tickle of bubbles as they rise to the surface. This is the immersive experience of the shallows. It's great, it's a mess and a tangle, and it exhilarates and sometimes takes your breath away.

If you really want to understand where you are, you need to move to somewhere calmer, somewhere where not quite as much is happening all at once. If you move to deeper water you will find things become still, less frenetic, and often more awe inspiring. When there isn't so much going on around you all at the same time you have the opportunity to focus, to examine in detail and understand rather than simply experience.

Living in the digital world can be dangerously like swimming in the shallows. While we often talk in education about the need to keep students "engaged" with their learning, we point to the vital importance of helping students disengage from this interconnected world for long enough to think more deeply and come to understand their own thinking. Our youngsters will have a far safer and more satisfying future if they know both how to stay connected and how to disconnect when necessary, giving themselves both the time and the space to examine the content of their own minds.

We need to build our own understanding of the digital world our kids live in so that we can help them explore its possibilities and guard against its dangers. We must empower them with the skills needed for the twenty-first century. We also need to reaffirm our status as the adults in this world, the grown-ups responsible for helping the younger generation develop a frame of mind and a set of skills that will ensure them a creative, compassionate, and effective adulthood.

A GIFT FOR THE FUTURE

The greatest gift we can give our young people, and humanity in general, is to ensure that we are raising a generation of effective thinkers. The advances of civilization over millennia have been the result of both great and innovative ideas, and of the ability of people to advance those great ideas in small, sometimes almost imperceptible steps. Civilizations hold together when people behave thoughtfully.

We are fond of saying "Don't just stand there, do something." The great educational writer and our mentor Dr Arthur Costa has pointed out the need sometimes to rephrase this as: "Don't just do something, stand there … and think."

- The world is changing.
- So are our children, and so are their brains.
- Technology is accelerating change in the world, in our children and in how we think.
- Problems will only be solved in this twenty-first-century digital age when we learn how to think in depth.
- The grown-ups need to lead the way and we will help you to do this.

Throughout the book there will be opportunities for the reader to think in greater depth in a specific area of focus—to pay closer attention to some of the bigger fish. We will also provide you with many examples of activities that help our youngsters to think deeply, to escape from information overload and think in the deep end.

🤿 We identify these opportunities with this symbol in the margin. This little diver is inviting you to think more deeply and to encourage youngsters to do more than just get "the gist" of something.

We also provide a set of questions at the conclusion of each chapter. These are designed to take your thinking beyond what you have just read and to see where it fits in your own context.

KEY IDEAS IN THIS CHAPTER

- Changes in the world are changing the ways we think.
- Our children are awash with information and stimulation.
- They are in danger of losing the ability to focus and think in depth.
- It is essential that we adults understand how the world has changed.
- We need to move away from seeing education as learning about "stuff."
- Our young people must learn how to be problem-solvers.

DISCUSSION

- What is your attitude toward new, digital technologies?
- How did you feel when you first discovered that mobile phones were equipped with cameras, that you could get an app that would order pizza and have it delivered to you?
- Do you ever feel intimidated by new technology? What are some of the things you have done to overcome that feeling?
- What are some of the greatest benefits of digital technology?
- What do you suspect are the problems?
- Where do you turn for information about a subject? Where did your parents turn?
- What are your major sources for news about what is happening in the world? Where do you think the young people you know get their news? How did your great grandparents find out about the world? How does this change things?
- Can you predict what changes you would see in your part of the world in twenty years' time?

Chapter Two

The World Is Changing

From Lines to Webs

More than forty-five years ago the Canadian professor and media philosopher Marshall McLuhan wrote these words (McLuhan, 2001):

> It is a matter of the greatest urgency that our educational institutions realize that we now have civil war among these environments created by media other than the printed word. The classroom is now in a vital struggle for survival with the immensely persuasive "outside" world created by new media. Education must shift from instruction, from imposing stencils, to discovery—to probing and exploration and to the recognition of the language of forms. The young today reject goals. They want roles. That is, total involvement. They do not want fragmented, specialized goals or jobs.

It is taking us a long time to understand the implications of what McLuhan described in his somewhat hyperbolic language as a "clash of cataclysmic proportions between two technologies." The technologies he speaks of are the technologies of the industrial, linear, print-orientated societies of the past and the new, interconnected, networked technologies of the digital and electronic age.

Let's look at this big fish and explore some deeper waters.

LINEAR THINKING

➤ We are moving from a society dominated by the printed word into the electronic age, where globalization and rapid communication of complex ideas are the order of the day. This is causing us to change the ways in which we think from predominantly linear modes to a more networked style of organic thinking. The emerging generation is thinking very differently from its predecessors, and the world they are creating will be different too. The problems of this new world will not be solved with the kinds of thinking we have been used to in the past. We need to break out of the linear modes of thinking to which we are accustomed.

As the prescient nineteenth-century Scottish American naturalist and philosopher John Muir told us, "When we try to pick out anything by itself, we find it hitched to everything else in the Universe."

The knowledge explosion of the twentieth and twenty-first centuries provides us with so much more information needing to be "hitched" to every other piece. But it goes much further than simply having vastly more bits of information to somehow integrate. The very act of "hitching" is changing in fundamental ways.

The development of the printing press by Gutenberg around 1440 changed the way people were thinking. It made the written language increasingly available to people, and its influence on thinking was pervasive. The printed language is linear, sequential, focused, and has permanence. Words are built up of letters representing sounds and these letters are placed in a linear sequence to form words. Words are then strung together in the same kind of sequence, one word after another, from left to right, each one following the previous word until we have a sentence. We mark the sentence as a separate entity by placing a small dot—a full stop or period. Then we begin the next sentence and it follows on from the previous one.

Good writing is characterized by fluency, the ease with which the sentences flow forward, one from another. The sentences build into paragraphs, paragraphs into chapters, and chapters into books. A book is the culmination of a long linear path taken one step at a time. We then place our books in libraries where they are ordered in linear fashion on horizontal shelves according to either a linear alphabetical system where A is followed by B or using a similarly linear numerical system such as the Dewey decimal system.

> The linear, sequential nature of print has had a powerful influence on thinking and the invention of the printing press changed the ways our plastic brains had operated prior to this domination of written language and the printed page.

We came to believe that effective thinking was characterized by a logical sequence of connected thoughts. Even more significantly, we came to think that this was the ONLY form of effective thinking. This linear path to good thinking is reflected in the comment "I don't follow you," made when we don't quite understand the argument. What we are saying is that we have lost the path, we cannot see, and hence we cannot follow the set of cognitive footsteps that is leading us toward a particular conclusion.

We have typically looked at intuition with great suspicion mainly because it doesn't follow the linear path, and it erupts with a kind of spontaneity from a underlying network of impressions, experiences, and "gut feelings" that are little understood in the logical, traditional senses of "understanding." But some of our greatest leaps of understanding have had their roots in this kind of nonlinear thinking. In spite of the predominance of linear thinking in the print age, we have always had the capacity for a different kind of thinking, thinking that seems to spring from the nonlinear and somewhat mysterious subconscious mind.

Einstein often reflected on his own problem-solving mind and saw something else at work (Suzuki, 1969):

> The theory of relativity occurred to me by intuition, and music is the driving force behind this intuition. My parents had me study the violin from the time I was six. My new discovery is the result of musical perception.

Linearity came to dominate our cultural lives in literate society. The keys of the piano are arranged in an alphabetical sequence from left to right, ABCDEFGABCDEFGABCDEFG, and so on. The classical musical score resembles the printed page of any book with rows of musical notation, taking the musician from page one to the end of the score along a predictable, linear, sequential path (see figure 2.1).

Figure 2.1

But jazz is a modern phenomenon and the jazz player doesn't create his music this way, and neither did primitive, preliterate man. The jazz pianist uses something more like intuition. He revisits phrases, circling back, spiraling down with a particular riff or phrase, interpreting and reinterpreting and probably never playing the same way twice. He listens to his "gut." Jazz has more in common with preliterate, preprint man than have the musical scores of the classical composers and musicians.

THE EXPERT, THE ARTIST, AND THE POINT OF VIEW

One of the things that literate, print-dominated culture did was create the notion of the single view point. Once a person's ideas could be written down in a book, they acquired a new kind of permanence and other people could refer to them even after the writer had died. We developed the concept of experts—the people who wrote the books. One person could sit, alone, with the thoughts of another profound thinker and hear those thoughts through the pages of a book. This is an amazing, culture-changing development and print made it possible.

We can see this striving for a logical, linear understanding of the world and the expression of a single view point in the art of the Age of Reason—the Renaissance. The understanding of the formal geometric principles of perspective had been growing in the west since the thirteenth and fourteenth centuries. By the early sixteenth century the painters of the Renaissance had largely mastered it.

Raphael's "School of Athens" was painted in 1509 and it is a perfect example. Everything in the painting is arranged according to a single view point, that of the artist. There is a single vanishing point and a single focus of interest around which everything else is arranged. Aristotle and Plato are engaged in deep, philosophical discussion, and Aristotle is holding a manuscript within which, presumably, are the recorded thoughts of the philosophers in logical, sequential, linear written language (see figure 2.2).

Having perfected the art of three-dimensional illusion in painting, many artists in the twentieth century have increasingly chosen to ignore it. Art has changed and continues to change. Just as primitive, preliterate man, drawing on cave walls, drew what he knew rather than what he saw, and was not directed by the rules of logic, perspective, or any single person's point of view, modern artists paint what they know and what they feel, often with little regard to literate notions of rationality. Compare Leonardo's sixteenth century Mona Lisa with this twentieth century cubist portrait (see figure 2.3).

Figure 2.2 The School of Athens, Raphael, 1509–1511.

Figure 2.3 Mona Lisa, Leonardo da Vinci, 1503.

The artist has managed to combine two completely different points of view into one image—profile and full face. Picasso's portrait of Marie-Therese Walter is a wonderful example of this new approach to point of view (see figure 2.4).

These changes have also filtered through the world of literature. The novel initially developed to tell a linear narrative that followed a fairly straight

Figure 2.4 Portrait of Marie-Terese Walter, Picasso, 1937.

forward temporal sequence from yesterday through today to tomorrow. If we plot the development with most classical works of fiction we can see a similar pattern—the exposition, a series of plot steps leading from one to the next and inexorably to some sort of climax. Following the climax we have another sequence of steps leading to a resolution and conclusion that nicely tie all the ends together—a final full stop.

Poetry too tended to fall into a regular, linear pattern. The English sonnet, for example, follows the pattern ABAB CDCD EFEF GG.

But things are changing dramatically in the world of literature. In the novel *Catch 22* by Joseph Heller, first published in 1961, we have a plot that is far from linear. Instead it is more like a spiral, constantly returning to the same event in the narrative and each time revealing a little more that helps us understand the protagonist Yossarian a little better. Modern poetry has strayed far from the formal structures of the sonnets and grown to encompass the visual elements of concrete poetry and a vast array of free form modes.

Even the movies have changed and we frequently find that the linear plot line has vanished and we walk away from the cinema with more questions than we had when we walked in and took our seats. In the movie *Vantage Point* we see the same event eight times, but each from a different point of view, and with each iteration we discover that our preconceptions were mistaken and misguided simply because of our previous point of view. Movies today are filled with flash backs, time shifts, multiple points of view, and unresolved conflicts.

THE PRINTED BOOK CHANGED IT ALL

The ability to write down a body of knowledge, to store it in a book, and to keep it in a library was a revolutionary development. It became possible for the first time to preserve the knowledge, the thoughts, and the experience of a single mind in a manner that could be referred to by future generations. The problem of "Chinese whispers" was eliminated. Passing on of knowledge in an oral culture was always hindered by the tendency for each repetition to contain the interpretations, the biases, and the coloration of the person entrusted with passage. Tiny changes became larger with each transmission. We do not know about Plato's philosophy other than through the writings of others, principally Aristotle, and so we are always inclined to wonder how far the translation from one mind to another, one language to another, and the passage of time might have changed the original meaning of Plato's philosophy.

> The advent of the book made it possible to build upon the findings and the ideas of earlier writers. This capacity for accurate, incremental growth in knowledge accelerated even further when the printing press made books more widely available to the populace.

The Wycliffe Bible was translated into Middle English between 1382 and 1395. This was closer to the language of the people than Latin, but very few people could read. The printing press had not yet been invented and so all books were handmade and so had very limited availability beyond the walls of the church and institutes of religious learning.

The printing press was invented around 1440, and between 1522 and 1534 Martin Luther translated the Bible into German, the language of the people, rather than leaving it in Latin, which had been accessible to only the priestly class. His mastery of the written language together with the increased availability of this Bible, thanks to the printing press, led to a powerful push for increased literacy. Luther wanted the ordinary people to be literate so they could read the Bible as it had been translated into their own, familiar language.

This flowering of literacy and the ready availability of the Bible to the literate population sowed the seeds of the Reformation. Thus began the gradual ascendancy of a new focus on the value of the individual human being and his powers of rational thought. These seeds of humanism eventually led to a system of laws that relied on evidence and rational argument. Scientific exploration blossomed and it was dependent on reason and evidence leading to a revolution in human thought. The days of the Inquisition were over because people had access to the Bible in their own homes. Every literate person could now interpret the teachings of their religion according to their own understandings of the original texts. The power of the clergy gave way to power of reason and the law. Eventually they also had access to the thinking of others over a broad range of subjects through the books they read and which were becoming more and more available to any literate person as the printing presses rolled.

Education became focused on reading. In universities one was said to be "reading" history, or physics, or whatever discipline had been selected for specialization. As each generation added to the knowledge and to the writings of the previous generation, the sheer quantity of information encouraged specialization. A superficial reading over a broad range of subjects left one open to the description of "Jack of all trades, master of none."

> Education encouraged study in depth and specialization, and this in turn led to the increasing separation of disciplines within the education system. Physics students did not tend to study music and history students were unlikely to know much about chemistry.

We know that polymaths have prospered in spite of this narrowing, but they tend not to be representative of the most common course of learning, a course that has led to greater and greater specialization. During the late fifteenth and early years of the sixteenth centuries Leonardo da Vinci was a scientist, mathematician, engineer, inventor, anatomist, painter, sculptor, architect, botanist, musician, and writer. More recently, we know that Albert Einstein was an accomplished musician as well as a theoretical physicist, and today the American Jared Diamond is an anthropologist, geographer, physiologist, author, and ornithologist. Today we tend to have neurologists and dermatologists, screen writers and writers for the live theater, poets and novelists, cellular biologists, electrical engineers, mechanical engineers, and computer engineers.

The Scientific Revolution, beginning with Galileo in the sixteenth century, contributed to this dramatic growth of knowledge. As information was collected it needed to be organized and categorized in order to make it accessible. This tended to lead to greater levels of fragmentation and categorization. We have reached a point in the twenty-first century where so much new research, so much new information, is being published daily that it is impossible for any one person to keep up even if that person is restricted to a single field of enquiry.

As Samuel Arbesman said in his article "Let's Bring the Polymath—and the Dabbler—Back" (*Wired* 12/13/13), "The most exciting inventions occur at the boundaries of disciplines, among those who can bring different ideas from different fields together." Enterprises that are on the cutting edge today encourage their idea developers to bridge the boundaries of specialization in their search for the next big thing or new idea.

AND THE INTERNET IS CHANGING IT ALL AGAIN

The development of the Internet is leading to some very significant changes in how we think of education and of learning in general. The Internet is not linear, it doesn't specialize, and its categories are loose and interconnected within a "World Wide Web." Webs are never straight lines.

The University of Melbourne was ranked twenty-eighth in the world in the Times Higher Education World University Rankings for 2012–2013 and has made significant and controversial changes to its degree structure with the "Melbourne Model." It used to be the case that upon entering the university a student was required to make a decision about the areas of specialization to be pursued over the next three or four years. Specialization was the order of the day.

This new model is tentatively moving away from this view of tertiary education and encouraging a greater degree of generalization and interconnectedness in learning. During the three undergraduate years the student is still expected to make a decision about whether to pursue studies in the arts, science, commerce, or another broad field of study. Within that field the student will focus on a major study, but also be encouraged to select from a wide range of subjects outside this major, to follow a passion unrelated to the focus of study, to explore a fascination or to work with students in a very different field of study, just as might be expected later in the workplace. Graduate degree programs are where the student engages in more intensive, focused, and job-oriented studies.

This move from specialization to generalization and the interrelationship and integration of learning is in part a response to the changing world of digital communication and knowledge availability. As young people interact with the Internet and experience the world as an interconnected, intricate web of ideas and information, our educational institutions have to change. We have to change to keep up.

Experiencing the search for information on the Internet is profoundly different from the experience we had when we headed to the pre-Internet library to learn about something. In a sense you needed to have already made up your mind about what it was you wanted to learn before you got to the library. How many times have you stood in a library and wondered where to begin?

Faced with rows and rows of books, and with basically only a linear search procedure at your disposal, the seeker of knowledge needed to have a focus in order to decide which section of library, indeed which shelf, will give him what he seeks. Libraries in the past were perfect examples of the linear, orderly arrangement of information. Each area of knowledge was grouped together and authors were arranged alphabetically.

The Internet is totally different, and libraries of today are changing rapidly because they recognize the need to accommodate this new interconnectivity. All that is needed in order to seek information on the Internet is a half-formed phrase or a couple of words. Type them into a favorite search engine and a world of possibilities opens up. From knowing almost nothing, from having not a clue about where to go next, Google and other search engines have opened an Aladdin's cave and you can sift, discard, and keep whatever you choose. It is virtually limitless. This sea of information is so vast and so deep it is easy to drown—or to avoid doing more than putting a toe in the water. We need to learn how to swim and to teach our children how to swim and stay safe in the deep end.

Networked bookmarking applications such as Diigo (https://www.diigo.com/) allow a person to accumulate, tag, and annotate web pages, making their own online, virtual "book." If one possible link interests you, you can click on it and begin to explore. But within that link there are hyperlinks that enable you to dig deeper and deeper until you are eventually—totally—lost. The options are never ending, the choices never cease, and everything is linked to everything else. Gone is the simple logic of the book written by an expert, with chapter building upon chapter and the whole offering a logically progressing point of view. This is the new world of interconnectedness and it requires a whole new set of navigational skills.

Crowd sourcing has become a powerful tool for innovation simply because it uses the interconnectivity of the Internet to bring together the minds of huge numbers of people and focuses them on a particular problem. In the search for the missing Malaysian airliner in 2014, the web site tomnod (http://www.tomnod.com/) had more than three million people painstakingly searching DigitalGlobe satellite images of the Southern Indian Ocean for debris. This web site was originally set up during a National Geographic project to find the tomb of Genghis Khan in the Valley of the Khans in Mongolia. Crowdsourcing also helped the United Nations High Commissioner for Refugees map the refugee populations in Somalia so that they knew where humanitarian help was most needed. Ground surveys were simply too dangerous, so satellite images were scoured by a global network of over 800 volunteers from more than 80 countries who mapped some 47,000 shelters in only 120 hours.

Furthermore, volunteer grid computing projects allow individuals to contribute their computer down time to advance computer projects. The first of these was SETI (Search for Extra Terrestrial Intelligence), which began in the 1960s. SETI makes use of this vast network of computers and analyzes the electromagnetic signals from space that are detected by radio telescopes. SETI has been replaced by the Berkeley Open Infrastructure for Networked Computing, which supports many other computing projects.

THE WORLD IS A SHAPE-SHIFTING PLACE

It was easy to predict where to find a particular book in a library if you understood the linear principles of its organization and you knew what you were looking for. Perhaps the most dramatic representation of this linear way of thinking outside of the library can be seen in the development of the assembly line, one of the highest achievements of the Industrial Revolution. Manufacture of everything was done one step at a time, each step modifying or adding to what came before. Ford installed one of the first assembly lines for the construction of motor cars. Working for Ford you might spend your life screwing a particular widget onto a particular nodger for eight hours each day.

Many companies have discovered that this linearity, this separation out into component parts that are simply added on to each other, may not be the best process for manufacture and increasingly teams working together to complete more complex phases of production. The most successful enterprises value creative thinking and the ability to work flexibly and think interdependently, because they know that their future prosperity lies there rather than having workers who are only skilled in the immediate task at hand.

Just one example of the changing scene is the digital printer, able to produce a three-dimensional object as a result of the directions of a computer. Today it is possible to produce a working, lethal firearm with one of these printers and no process workers. Perhaps tomorrow this is how we will build cars. Scientists are able to print body parts in the laboratory and are working to find ways of perfecting these techniques so that we can have a supply of replacements when our own body parts become damaged or simply wear out.

We have been traditionally educated to fit an outdated industrial model. Our schools lead us from one grade level to the next, our days are divided into lessons that followed in sequence from one to the next, and our progress is checked on by tests measuring the modifications and additions to each student as he or she progresses along the assembly line we called education.

If the world no longer works this way we had better start working to understand how it does work.

THE WORLD AND OUR BRAINS ARE NOT AS WE THOUGHT

The more we learn about the brain and how it functions, the more we come to realize that it is an intricate, interactive network—a bit like the Internet but even more complex. We need to develop a system of teaching that reflects both the new world in which we live and our growing understanding of the brain with which we learn. We need to reorganize learning so that it utilizes all of its sensory information in order to take advantage of the brain's natural modus operandi and strengthen its neural networks.

The educational model we have inherited is not just highly differentiated into sequential year levels and subject disciplines; it is also primarily linear, verbal, and a mixture of visual and auditory. Most teaching and learning involves being told or by reading, and most processing requires a student to retell or write. This does not fit with what we now know about the brain and the dynamic, multisensory, plastic ways in which it operates, ways that are more analogous to the dynamic, interconnected world of the Internet than to the linear production line.

The speed, complexity, and nonlinearity of electronic media are changing the ways we think. Media shrinks both time and space. We have the ability to see, know, and participate in events all over the globe as they are happening. In Africa, Europe, Asia, Australia, and the Americas, we can all simultaneously watch a sporting event, a concert, or a developing news story as it is happening, all together. And while it is happening we can express and share our thoughts and responses using platforms such as Facebook and Twitter.

We can all have a voice. We are immersed in a continuous flow of ever-changing information. Pattern recognition is becoming more important than simple data collection and classification, in large part because of the sheer volume of data available to us. We are experiencing rapid social and cultural change because we are being changed in fundamental ways by these new electronic and digital media.

The global scale and the speed of economic and financial transactions during the late twentieth and early twenty-first centuries outstripped our capacity to "follow" what was going on and predict what would happen next—leading to the Global Financial Crisis. Digital reading, Wikipedia, Facebook, Twitter, and the Arab Spring are all manifestations of this change in the ways in which people think. Libraries are being created that have no books made of paper. Everything is available, and only available, digitally. Opinions propagate and morph at incredible speed as they are accessed, altered, and spread across the Internet. Today we can see new industries and products taking off with the support of crowdfunding.

A recent study of over one billion Facebook status updates was undertaken by John Fowler (a University of California, San Diego professor of medical genetics and political science) and others. They revealed the potential for social media to spread even our moods across the globe. This study discovered that for every post with either a positive or a negative emotional tone we see, an additional one to two similarly toned messages will be posted by others elsewhere in the world. "These results imply that emotions themselves might ripple through social networks" (Coviello et al., 2014).

We also see this new way of thinking about and experiencing the world reflected in literature, film, theater, and the visual arts. The rise of "New Age" thinking revels in mystery and the apparent rejection of logic as the only acceptable way of examining the world. This acceptance intuition and a focus on connectedness and group responsibility are signs of both a return to some of the ways of thinking that characterized preliterate societies and signs of new ways of interacting with reality.

THIS DIGITAL, INTERCONNECTED GENERATION THINKS DIFFERENTLY

One might argue that this is not the only era of massive technological change. Anyone born in the early 1900s would have experienced communities transformed through the widespread introduction of electricity and the electric light. Flush toilets, telephones, cars, a radio in every home, television, and the increasing availability of commercial air travel transformed our way of life and transformed us.

What is different now is the speed of change. One has only to look at the rate of new mobile phone generations; each change is marked by comprehensive transformations in the information-processing technology. Consider how rapidly we have progressed through one groundbreaking advance after another in television receivers. In 1965, Gordon Moore, President and CEO of INTEL, estimated the growth of semiconductor computing capacity to double every eighteen months. Despite the fact that this estimate was based on very sparse data, it holds true today and is called "Moore's Law."

The problem is one of keeping up with this rapidly changing, and for most of us, unpredictable, digital technology. Who knows what Google Glass or digital printing might mean for us in five years? We are entering an era of technologically induced unemployment where, more and more frequently, human jobs are being taken over by digital technology. ATM machines, automatic pumps at the petrol station, self-checkouts at the supermarket, and robotic assembly lines have replaced many of the unskilled jobs of the past. Robotic vehicles stack and retrieve from huge warehouses and digital systems maintain the inventory. The old jobs are going and the future will belong to those who can adapt and innovate—to the thinkers.

When you look at the children in your school it is important to try and understand how different the world they are growing up is from the world in which you grew up. Some of their parents may be avid users of social media and search engines, as you may be, and others may still be unsure and tentative when using computers and the Internet. Some parents fear this digital world and don't know how best to protect their children, let alone help them make best use of the powerful tool that it is.

These children who seldom watch only one screen at a time, who are texting and googling as they watch television, and who hardly ever email but instead send abbreviated 140-character messages with thumbs that seem to flash across the virtual keyboards on their phones think differently from you and you think differently from their grandparents. Their plastic brains are being wired differently by this new technology as they experience the world through that technology. They no longer want to do one thing at a time unless it totally grips and engages them. They are connected with one another and the world digitally through most of their waking hours.

Many of them find it tough to begin reading a book at page one and then progress, one page at a time, through the linear sequence of plot or argument. Their thoughts play more like jazz than classical music, they riff and improvise constantly. They value intuition and gut feeling as much, if not more, than carefully reasoned logic. They seek powerful experiences that stimulate in multiple directions all at once. They are attracted to things in the world that move and change constantly rather than the quiet contemplation of one thing at a time.

In other words, youngsters today are often captivated and sometimes confused by the sheer quantity of information and information sources. They are distracted by the excitement and variety that surround them in the shallows. At first sight, the world of the shallows seems more than enough for them. Our task is to help them into the deep end where the water is calm, and where they can find the big fish—the big ideas.

This nonlinear, interwoven, networked, ever-changing, rapid fire world is a shape shifter. Many of the old progressions, and the predictability that went with them, have become irrelevant. There is less and less that they can be sure of—including the old chestnut that a good education will get them a good, secure job, a career for life.

Do not underestimate the difficulty of a task such as this, when the *Common Core State Standards: Science and Technical Subjects Grades 6–8* states that students should be able to

> Follow precisely a multistep procedure when carrying out experiments, taking measurements, or performing technical tasks: CCSS.ELA-LITERACY.RST.6–8.3

We are asking students to operate in a purely linear, multistep fashion when they live within a networked environment with which they are very familiar. We are asking them to do something alien to the way they increasingly experience the world. These young people live in a world of "all at onceness" and we will have to teach them how to disengage from that world in order to focus, step by step, on these linear procedures that are so important.

We have to make sure that we keep the baby AND the bathwater. Linear thinking is powerful. Our task is to ensure that we exploit the opportunities for learning that the digital world provides without losing the capacity to think in linear, carefully focused ways. We need to cultivate both.

Teachers need to understand these changes in the world, in our experience of the world, and in our understandings about how the brain works. We also need to help parents and the broader community understand them too. Only then can we continue to be the grown-ups and give our kids the support they need to navigate this digital world and make use of its enormous richness and power for the betterment of themselves within society.

KEY IDEAS IN THIS CHAPTER

- Technology has moved us from the linear, print-oriented societies that culminated in the Industrial era into the interconnected, networked societies in which we now live.
- We can see these changes in many aspects of our culture—in music, in art, in the structure of the book, the development of "experts," and the growth of specialization.
- Now we can see that traditional libraries are giving way to electronic sources of information.
- We are awash with information and connected with others across the globe.
- Many educational institutions are moving away from specialization and toward more integrated curricula.
- In both education and industry there is a move toward working cooperatively in groups.
- The world has changed and is continuing to change at an increasingly rapid rate.
- It is important that we don't forget the power of focused linear thinking in depth.

DISCUSSION

- Make a list of activities that characterize your professional life. Try and divide them into two groups—one group will contain the things that are essentially linear in nature, the other those things that are more diffused and interconnected.
- Where have you experienced this move away from the purely linear in your cultural life—movies, art, literature, television, music?
- What do you think your students know to do with digital technology that you cannot do?
- How can you make good use of this knowledge gap if you find one?
- How do the predictions you were able to make for your own life differ from the predictions you can make about the lives of your students?
- Do you see the development of curriculum design in your school moving toward greater specialization or greater integration? How do you feel about that in the light of this discussion?

Chapter Three

Surveying the Landscape
Education and Learning

We use a lot of analogies. Robert Marzano tells us that analogies help us understand complex material by relating what is new to something we already know and exploring them by the things they have in common (Marzano, 2001). It also helps to engage both the visual imagination and sensory memory. Good teachers do this all the time.

Do you like to travel? We travel a lot and have done so for much of our adult lives. Let's consider two different kinds of travelling.

One is filled with surprises because we know virtually nothing of the landscape or the history of the place we are visiting. Every new vista, every new city is greeted with lots of "ooh's and ahhh's" as we discover things we had not expected. At the end of the trip we have a marvelous collection of memories and photographs. The trouble is that these memories and images are rather like a kaleidoscope—fascinating, changing glimpses but lacking any clear pattern. The colors enchant, but how do they fit together?

The other kind of travelling involves either doing some homework first or drawing on the knowledge we might already have of the places we are planning to visit. Having completed an undergraduate degree in Fine Arts with a focus in the final year on the Renaissance in Italy provided a rich background against which to visit Rome, Florence, Milan, and Ravenna. These were the important places to visit because past study had revealed their centrality to the development of painting, sculpture, and architecture during the early to late Renaissance period.

Before visiting Hawaii for an extended period, we read James Michener's semifictional novel "Hawaii." It served as a kind of conceptual map, a broad brush impression of the historical, physical, and social landscape we were about to explore. Living there for three months we began to discriminate more accurately between the fictional and factual elements of his story and to amplify and enrich our initial impressions of Hawaii.

This latter kind of travelling provides something more abiding than the collage of recollections that remain from our unprepared travels. It leads to a deeper understanding of the place rather than simply a collection of fascinating and vivid but often superficial and disconnected impressions.

HOW DO YOU SOLVE A PROBLEM?

To solve a complex problem you need to understand the context within which the problem exists. We are about to explore a complex set of ideas about our changing digital society, as it has come to be, and about how our children can best thrive within it. If we are to understand the places we are going to visit, and end up with more than a kaleidoscopic collage of impressions, we need some context and an appreciation of how we got to where we are now.

This chapter examines the cultural, pedagogical, and scientific advances that have led to our present understandings about learning and about education. As we try to make sense of current practices we will dive more deeply in order to understand the past upon which the present rests and out of which the practices of the future will grow.

We ask that you persevere, because this is serious stuff with which we are dealing. It's important that we understand rather than simply collect a set of superficial impressions.

Some of these may be very familiar to you. Most teachers have learned about the various theories of learning during their training. What we are doing in this chapter is setting the stage for the rest of the book by reviewing learning theories from a particular point of view, placing them in a context that reflects the themes of the book—that the world is changing, becoming more interconnected and more complex, and we need to understand these complexities if we are to function optimally within it.

> Questions that begin with "how" and "why" are like the weights that divers use to help them to escape the surface. They help us think a bit more deeply.

How did our notion of "education" develop? Why do we define it in the ways we do?

> What do we understand about how our children learn? How has our understanding of "learning" changed and grown? Learning and education are very big fish indeed.

The profound changes wrought by the digital age occur within the context of our understandings about "education" and about "learning," so it is a worthwhile journey to explore what we mean by both of these concepts.

We all have a general idea about the meanings of these terms, but trying to tie them down can be a bit like swimming in the shallows—lots of fleeting impressions rather than any deeper understanding.

EDUCATION—WHERE HAVE WE BEEN? WHERE ARE WE GOING?

So how did we get to where we are now? All over the world societies are agonizing over test scores on international comparison instruments such as PISA (Programme for International Student Assessment carried out by the OECD), TIMSS (Trends in International Mathematics and Science Study), and PIRLS (Progress in International Reading and Literacy Study). They worry about how many of their kids are dropping out of school, whether the quality of education is declining and why kids are becoming disengaged. Above all they are worried about how well we are preparing them to live rewarding and satisfying lives when they finally leave school. We are engaged in a global competition and every government in the developed world is trying to shuffle the odds to get a winning spot.

WHAT DO WE MEAN BY "EDUCATION?"

The notion of a "good" education has been discussed since the ancient Greeks. As early as the seventh century BCE, the fathers of poor boys were urged to ensure their sons received an education at home that fitted them for a trade. The children of the more well to do were provided with a well-rounded education in numeracy, literacy, physical education, and the arts. An educated population was seen as the foundation for a successful democracy. Slaves, laborers, and often women tended to be left out of education because they were not deemed to be a part of democratic decision making. Things were a little different in ancient Sparta where women were educated because they were expected to take over the running of the city state when the men were at war. In general, though, the women learned about running a household, bringing up children and tending to their men folk from their own mothers.

Socrates, in the fifth century BCE, is reported to have said "I cannot teach anybody anything. I can only make them think." The distinction between learning "stuff" and being educated was already understood. In Socrates' view, education was about the whole child, the intellect, the body, the imagination, and the soul.

Even before Socrates, the Greek philosopher Thales asked: "What man is happy? He who has a healthy body, a resourceful mind and a docile nature." We might argue over the "docile nature," but not the notion of "*mens sana in corpore sano*" the healthy mind in a healthy body also described by the Roman poet Juvenal. Games and poetry were as important as the development of a spirit of enquiry to both the ancient Greeks and the Romans.

As the centuries rolled on, the place of education in society has had many shifts and transformations. During the first thousand years of the Christian era, very few in Britain had any formal education at all. That doesn't mean, of course, that there was no learning taking place. The son of the blacksmith learned from his father at the forge. At first he would simply watch and probably ask interminable questions, but as he became more capable he might be asked to fetch things, hold things, or even take over some of the simpler tasks.

By watching the master craftsman and imitating him over time, the young boy gradually grew into a blacksmith who was now able to add his own techniques and preferences to the skills of the iron worker. In the kitchen the young girl watched as her mother made bread, following the same pattern of observation, gradual participation, and adaptation until she had made the skill her own.

The development of medieval trade created a need for the merchants and trades people in the growing towns to become more educated. Town life was more complicated and trading across the far reaches of Europe and even Asia required record keeping and the ability to read and write. Education was becoming a utilitarian necessity and as education spread more and more widely over the coming centuries, its focus on utilitarian uses became more and more entrenched. The commercial enterprise required good record keeping and accountancy, and this combined with the exchange of ideas following travel increased the pace of development in both mathematical and language learning.

The Industrial Revolution had an even more powerful influence on learning and education. The growth of factories required a work force that knew how to count and calculate, to read instructions, and write reports. It also needed people who knew how to follow instructions and do as they were told. The development of schools to meet these needs followed and one might observe that this model still holds true today, even in postindustrial societies.

In twenty-first-century developed nations it is still a commonly held belief that the central business of schools is to teach children how to behave, how to read and write, and to be able to do basic mathematics. With such a view of education it comes as no surprise that various testing regimes including No Child Left Behind in the United States, the National Assessment Program—Literacy and Numeracy (NAPLAN), and the assessment of the National Curriculum in the United Kingdom focus their attentions on mathematics and literacy.

HOW DO WE UNDERSTAND "LEARNING"?

Before the Industrial Revolution the lives children led were not all that different from the lives led by their parents. A father would teach his son a trade and how to provide for and protect his family. A mother would teach her daughter the skills needed to maintain the household and raise a family. The situation is certainly very different today. The world our children will inherit is vastly different from that of their parents. Since we cannot predict the problems our children and students will face or what skills they will need to solve them, we must think carefully about how we teach them and prepare them for an uncertain future.

Gender roles have become far less distinct, employment options and patterns are changing dramatically, and the very concept of "family" is undergoing significant change in developed countries. The rapid development of technology is changing the workplace and the play place.

You might be surprised to discover that in many ways we don't seem to have progressed much further in our organization of schooling since the latter days of the Industrial Revolution despite the vast changes that have taken place in society. Society has always endeavored to teach our children the skills needed to survive and to thrive. But as environments change so do these skills. We no longer need to teach our boys how to hunt down a bison or build a fire stick. In economically developed societies our girls don't need to learn how to weave baskets or form and fire clay pots. Instead, our children need to know how to navigate the aisles in Walmart and how to shop safely online.

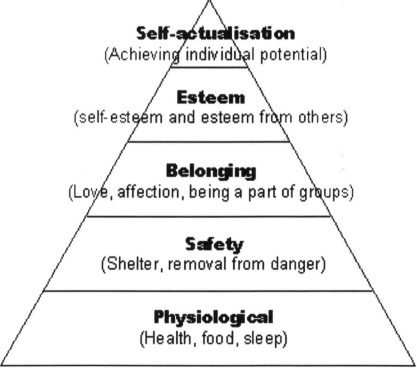

Figure 3.1 Maslow's Pyramid Depicts a Hierarchy of Human Needs. The Base of the Pyramid Shows the Most Fundamental Needs (from www.changingminds.org).

Chapter Three

THE GROWING SCIENCE OF LEARNING

Let's do some thinking about how we have got to our present understanding about people learn.

During the twentieth century we developed a science of learning that created a much clearer picture of how our children learn things and how adults continue to learn. The focus moved from being almost entirely about how we should teach people, to a growing understanding of how people learn. The National Research Council (NRC) in the United States published *How People Learn: Bridging Research and Practice* in 1999 after a two-year study by the Committee on Developments in the Science of Learning. A year later an expanded version was published entitled "How People Learn: Brain, Mind, Experience and School." Since then *How Students Learn: History, Mathematics and Science in the Classroom* (2005) and *Preparing Teachers: Building Evidence for Sound Policy* (2010) have all been published by the NRC.

This research has all placed the emphasis firmly on the learner first. Until we understand how learning takes place we will be unable to design teaching that will be truly successful. The learner must take pride of place rather than the teacher.

There were four major routes to this growing understanding of learning. Understanding where we are now requires an understanding of these pathways—where they originated and how they intermingle.

Behaviorism

Behaviorism was one of the first of these. Parents had watched their children learn by trial and error and understood that they continued to learn new things in the same manner. If we touch something hot, it hurts, and so we are less likely to do it again because the stimulus of that first hot thing we touched led to the anticipation of pain should we touch a hot object again.

Ivan Pavlov was a Russian physiologist born in 1849 and he named this explanation of learning Behaviorism. He had been studying the digestive processes of dogs but noticed something unexpected. The dogs would begin to salivate when they heard the signal that they were about to be fed—the ringing of a bell. This became far more interesting to him than the process of digestion and so he turned his attention to the study of a behavior he named "classical conditioning." He showed that when feeding of the dogs was preceded by some coincidental event, such as the ringing of a bell, the dogs would eventually become conditioned to salivate whenever they heard a bell, regardless of the presence of food.

This is a straightforward and simple explanation of some forms of learning and we have all experienced it. The American psychologist B. F. Skinner took Pavlov's ideas further. He argued that we behave as we do in part because certain behaviors are either rewarded or punished. One of Skinner's most famous experiments involved a pigeon in a box. Inside the box there was a lever and if the pigeon pecked the lever it would receive a small pellet of food. Without the reward of food the pigeon may rarely if ever peck the lever, but having pecked it once and discovered the consequential reward, the pigeons became expert lever peckers. They became so expert, in fact, that they would eventually continue to peck the lever even when their rewards stopped coming.

Kids are not pigeons, but much of our understanding of how to manage their behavior derives from the descriptions of conditioning developed by behaviorists such as Pavlov and Skinner.

We need to consider carefully how we condition children to behave, in particular by the ways in which we use rewards and punishments. A reward for a child can be anything from a new toy, to a smile, a hug, or an approving glance. Conditioning can be a means of developing and eventually habituating desired behaviors. It can also be used in more subtle ways to develop attitudes and sets of beliefs. The small child who receives approval for acts of generosity is more likely to develop into a generous adult.

On the other hand, the child who senses negativity from his parents toward his friendships with children from different racial groups is more likely to develop racist tendencies as an adult. The tragic truth that homosexual adolescents are more likely to self-harm than heterosexual youngsters demonstrates the power of negative reinforcement in the development of both attitudes and self-worth.

Perhaps most critically we need to consider how we use praise. Praise is a powerful reward for children. If we praise children for things into which they have put no effort—such as being cute, having big brown eyes, getting an A on a test for which they did not need to study—then we are reinforcing a behavior that says, "I value myself for my innate qualities, rather than how hard I work or how much effort I put in." If, on the other hand, we praise children for the amount of effort they put into a task, we are reinforcing a belief in themselves that grows out of effort. To reward a child for things that require no effort is a risky prospect. It is clear which kind of conditioned behavior is most likely to lead to a productive and satisfying life.

Cognitivism

Cognitive psychologists have added a great deal to our understanding of learning by adopting a view that the mind is like a kind of "black box" that should be opened and explored. Human mental processes such as thinking, understanding, creativity, memory, and problem-solving began to be studied and the understanding gained has been incorporated in various ways into theories of child rearing and instructional programs in our schools.

Linguist Noam Chomsky (Chomsky, 2002) pointed out that a learning theory (like behaviorism) that only takes into account stimuli and responses is insufficient to explain the extraordinary complexity inherent in the learning of language. A child who cannot add two and two, who cannot even tie his own shoe laces, is able to construct an original, grammatically correct sentence. This sentence has a subject, a verb that agrees with the subject, a personal pronoun placed in just the right place, an object, and the number of which agreed with the indefinite article "a."

The child knows when to use the definite article (the) and when to use the indefinite article "a," as well as selecting an interrogative intonation pattern, all of this in the sentence: "Can I have a banana please?" Chomsky believed that internal mental structures must also play a role. The uncovering of these mental structures became a focus for researchers and educators alike.

The organization of things to be learned was another important area of research and consideration. It might seem obvious that arranging tasks to be learned from simple to complex should facilitate learning. Start with the easy stuff and get progressively more difficult. Children begin their mathematical learning by counting objects and progress, step by step, with increasing complexity and understanding, to calculus.

But this isn't quite as straightforward as it seems for all forms of learning. How did you learn to ride a bicycle? What was the early, easy part? Was it learning how to balance, the coordination of two pedaling feet, or the manipulation of the handlebars? For most people, learning to ride a bicycle involved getting on one, maybe falling off a few times, but basically doing the whole deal, all at once, with gradually growing sophistication.

We have misrepresented the teaching of reading for generations of young children by trying to fit it into a lockstep, hierarchical model. We believed that if we began with individual letters, then put them together into simple words, then into sentences, and finally into paragraphs and chapters, children would easily learn to read. The trouble is that reading is a language process and we don't learn language like this. We know, for instance, that one of the first things babies learn about language is intonation patterns. They babble questions, comments, complaints, and conversations long before they know any words.

The Australian reading researcher Brian Cambourne was once heard to comment that if we taught children to talk in the same hierarchical, lockstep fashion we tried to teach them to read, we would have a generation of mute children.

It isn't easy to organize knowledge hierarchically, but that doesn't mean it isn't sometimes helpful to try. For some kinds of learning it works very well. For more complex learning it can be misleading.

Charles Reigeluth and his Elaboration Theory and Benjamin Bloom and his Taxonomy of Learning have both been leading thinkers in the attempt to organize knowledge. Bloom developed, and others have revised, a classification of thinking that moves from less to more complex in the following manner:

> *Remembering:* I remember the date of the Battle of Hastings was 1066.
> *Understanding:* I understand what happened during the Battle of Hastings.
> *Applying:* I can apply my understanding of the Battle of Hastings in order to create a timeline of events.
> *Analyzing:* I can identify the historical trends that led up to the battle.
> *Synthesize:* I can bring to bear what I know about the Battle of Hastings and World War Two and see the similarities and differences.
> *Evaluate:* I can compare the two conflicts and make a judgment about how much we have learned in the intervening years.

This view of learning took the emphasis away from a focus on how best to *teach* something to a new focus on how we *learn* something. The learner became the key player in the investigation, rather than the teacher. Learning was now seen as something that children do, rather than as something we do to children.

If you walk into any school in the western world you are likely to see some version of Bloom's taxonomy displayed on the wall or incorporated into teachers' planning. But it too is only a part of the picture and can often be misleading because learning does not seem to follow any straightforward progression from simple to complex. Learning can be highly recursive, and it is invariably interconnected, dynamic, and organic.

Constructivism

Constructivism argues that learning is a process of development and construction and builds on the theories of the cognitivists. Each stage of learning builds on what went before and the learner actively processes new information in the light of what is already known.

The Swiss psychologist Jean Piaget (1896–1980) also provided an organizational structure for learning. He based his organizational structure on the development of the child rather than on the apparent complexity of the kinds of thinking involved in learning. He observed children as they attempted to understand the world they lived in and he suggested that children go through four stages of cognitive development, each stage building on what had been learned in the preceding stage.

Piaget described the period from birth to around two years of age as the Sensory Motor Stage. During this stage babies are learning about their environments. They come to recognize all the objects and people around them and they discover that they can have a degree of control over some things and not others. They also begin to develop a sense of their own identity.

From two to seven years of age Piaget observed that children begin to organize their environments and classify things. He named this the preoperational stage when children deal with things in different groups differently although, according to Piaget, they are not yet able to think abstractly. While a child at this stage may know quite clearly that a particular truck belongs to him, he will not have a generalized sense of "ownership" and this can become very clear when he wants to take another child's truck and make it his own too. Learning during this stage is best done with concrete objects and direct experiences.

During the years seven to eleven, children enter what Piaget called the Concrete Operational Stage. As children progress in their ability to deal with concrete objects and situations they begin to think abstractly about them. As their ability for abstraction and conceptual thought develops, they become able to make logical connections to explore and explain their encounters with the world.

The final stage of development comes during the years of eleven to sixteen when children are able to think without concrete objects. Piaget calls this period the Formal Operational Stage. Youngsters are able to argue in the abstract, to consider a proposition, and evaluate its validity. They can reason deductively. This stage is embodied in the thinking of an adult.

The importance of Piaget's contribution was the stratification of development into plausible stages. His descriptions of the stages of development enabled teachers to develop classroom experiences that reflected these stages.

The growing understanding of the learner was beginning to exercise a more influential role in the development of curriculum and teaching practice.

Critics have suggested that Piaget underestimated the capacities of young children. We also know from the kinds of recent brain studies that were not available to Piaget and his confreres that some areas of the human brain are not fully developed until the early twenties. The range of Piaget's stages could easily be extended by a decade. Furthermore, the neuroplasticity of the brain indicates that the process of thinking formally can improve throughout life.

What is important, however, is that our view of what was most important in teaching and learning was changing, and the focus was shifting away from the curriculum and the teacher and more toward the learner.

Humanism

Humanism places learning within the context of social and human needs. Abraham Maslow (1908–1970) recognized that it was essential to meet basic human needs if learning is to take place affectively. He described these fundamental human needs by reference to a hierarchical pyramid with the most basic needs at the bottom. The satisfaction of these needs, according to Maslow, underlies all human behavior including all learning, whether formal or informal (see figure 3.1).

Our most fundamental needs are physiological and related to our successful biological survival. We need food, shelter, fresh air to breathe, and the opportunity to reproduce and secure the continuation of our kind. Above that, Maslow sees our need for safety. We need to feel secure from threats and believe we are able to protect ourselves and those we hold dear.

The next level in the hierarchy is the need for a sense of belonging. We are social beings and we need to feel accepted and a part of a group. Even further up the pyramid comes the need for self-esteem. Maslow says we need to feel that we are valuable, and we need to think well of ourselves. Only when all of the foundational levels of the pyramid are in place can we feel "self-actualized."

The need for esteem—the esteem of others as well as self-esteem—is a basic human need and this is why the use of praise is such a powerful stimulus to learning. We discuss this in a later chapter in some detail because it has been a contentious and sometimes disruptive element in the debates over child rearing and education over recent decades.

As we attempt to deal with the underachievement of children growing up in generational poverty, we understand more keenly the importance of the human element in education. The child who comes to school hungry or sleep deprived, who fears that his family may be evicted from their apartment, will not learn effectively.

While we may understand the behaviorist underpinnings of learning, we may cater for the developmental stage of the child in designing classroom activities, and we may ensure that each new learning experience builds on previous learning, and if Maslow's list of basic human needs are not met, effective learning will not take place.

Some Other Views of Learning

The development of our understanding of how children learn continues to be a rich and fertile ground. Each of the pathways we have just explored has added to our understanding and ability to explore the terrain. We see the interweaving of the work of the behaviorists who analyzed the behavior of animals and humans, the cognitivists who wanted to understand the intricacies of the human mind, the constructivists who explored how we build up meaning and understanding through our experiences, and the humanists who set all this in the context of basic human needs. But we are not done quite yet. There are still some more tracks to be discovered. Let's look at a few of them.

John Dewey (1859–1952), a philosopher and social activist with an abiding interest in education. He argued that school is a social institution as well as an instrument for social change and believed that learning should prepare students to think imaginatively and innovatively about the experiences they will encounter. He thought that students thrived when allowed to participate in their own learning, stressing the importance of relating new knowledge to an individual student's prior knowledge—a somewhat prescient view of learning given that he died over sixty years ago.

Jerome Bruner (1915–2016) founded the Centre for Cognitive Studies at Harvard University. He could be described as both a cognitivist and a humanist. He proposed a spiral model of learning wherein the learner revisited what was already known, but each time adding to its depth and complexity. His view of learning was not dissimilar to that of Vygotsky whom we mention a little further on, and is strongly reflected in the work of Lane Clark.

He also saw a powerful social and cultural element in all learning. Bruner believed that social interactions were an integral part of all learning and thinking. In particular he believed that children learn language within a social parent-and-child context, and that the quality of that interaction significantly influences the quality of the learning. Bruner also believed that the most effective learning took place when the learner was motivated by an interest in the subject matter rather than by extrinsic rewards and punishments such as test marks and awards.

Lane Clark. While Bloom's taxonomy has become a standard for the organization of knowledge, there are other educators, such as Lane Clark, who argue that while the categories are fine, they are not necessarily hierarchical. She believes that thinking, which is at the heart of learning, is not hierarchical and does not exist in levels of complexity. Instead, she argues that all levels of thinking are interrelated and that we cycle in a kind of spiral between the levels, bringing each in as it is needed and as it adds to a growing understanding of what we are learning. As new learning is incorporated into prior learning, we are always constructing meanings and building understandings. This process never ends.

Lev Vygotsky (1896–1934). We have not yet looked at the influence society has on learning. To ignore this would be a huge omission because we are such social beings. It's here that we turn to a Belarusian psychologist whose work remained unknown in the West until the late 1960s. Vygotsky studied the higher-level cognitive development in children.

Vygotsky believed that the child's social milieu was vital to his learning and he saw development emerging from social interactions. In the process of gaining knowledge from another person, let's say the teacher, the learner makes a transition from an initial state that requires the teacher's guidance, to a final state where the learner is able to think and act independently. Parents, teachers, and society at large are vital, in Vygotsky's view, because they provide the environment, the knowledge, and the skills the child will learn as well as the scaffolding that will enable the learner to internalize that learning and make it his own.

Vygotsky has helped us to see much more clearly the influences of the family and the community on children's learning and development. If the social environment and supports are not conducive to the child, learning and then his development will be at risk. Much of the work on children growing up in extreme poverty relies on his findings and of those who followed him, including the English educational sociologist Basil Bernstein and, perhaps more contentiously, the work of Ruby Payne in the United States.

Howard Gardner has written extensively about the concept of multiple intelligences—that we can be intelligent in many different ways, making any single measure of intelligence a misrepresentation of the complexity of the human mind.

Carol Dweck is working hard to drag us out of the era of unearned praise and self-esteem into a new paradigm that links praise to effort and places its faith in the ability of the brain to grow new neurons and make new connections when we work hard at a difficult task.

Arthur Costa and Bena Kallick examined the behaviors engaged in by successful people in a wide range of contexts. They were particularly interested in uncovering what it is that good thinkers do when they are faced with problems where the answer is not readily apparent. They developed a list of sixteen Habits of Mind, the dispositions and behaviors that will be most likely to support the effective and efficient use of the various thinking skills we might employ.

Many other thinkers and researchers have written about the relationship between language, thinking, and learning, including Noam Chomsky, William Labov, Basil Bernstein, Gordon Wells, and others. If you are interested in reading more we have placed a reading list at the back of this book.

Today there are vast numbers of books available about how we learn. A search on Amazon reveals more than half a million and more are being tapped out on keyboards right now. Regardless of their similarities and differences, they will all have grown out of the theories we have briefly reviewed as they gradually came to appreciate the marvelous richness and complexity of the human mind and how it learns.

> Learning is neither linear nor straightforward. It is a shape-shifting process, and educators need to be nimble and flexible enough in order to move with it.

HOW WELL DO WE UNDERSTAND THE "BIG FISH" OF LEARNING AND EDUCATION?

Each set of theories has given us a particular viewpoint and just as any landscape is seen only partially from just one viewpoint, each of these has enabled us to see more of the actual lay of the land. Behaviorists and cognitivists have explored the workings of the human mind and seek to organize both the things that need to be learned and the stages by which we learn them.

Constructivism puts a particular kind of spin on these workings telling us that learning is a building project in which the learner is actively involved in processing new information, slotting it in with prior knowledge and building new levels of understanding. The learner is not a blank slate but brings an increasingly rich store of personal experiences to learning. We must then add to this the fact that we are social beings and that society has a powerful role to play in all learning.

The development of learning theories has been analogous to the creation of pieces of a jigsaw puzzle. It is only when we begin to organize the multitude of pieces that we can see the whole picture. Sometimes our ways of organizing may not be perfect and we may need to rejig the placement of the pieces. It is certainly the case that we don't yet have all the pieces in our possession. Organization is helpful as long as we don't make it into a rigid, unalterable structure.

Don't glue the jigsaw down until you are sure you have the whole picture completed.

KEY IDEAS IN THIS CHAPTER

- It's important to understand what we mean by "learning" and by "education."
- Our understandings about both have become more complex and intertwined as we have learned more.

- The Industrial Revolution had a powerful influence on our notion of "education"—children should be taught to behave, to be literate and numerate in order to work in factories.
- The science of "learning" has grown over time and become more complex.
- Each development in our understanding of how we learn has grown out of and added to previous beliefs.
- Four major strands in our understanding have been: behaviorism, cognitivism, constructivism, and humanism.
- Others have added to these four strands.
- We now understand that learning is frequently not linear. Learning is a complex interactive process within the individual's brain and within society.
- We still have a lot to learn about learning.

DISCUSSION

- Can you find examples in your own recent practice that shed light on each of these different views of education?
- Have any particular theories of learning had more influence on you than others?
- Does education only happen in schools? What examples can you give of significant education that happens outside the formal school setting?
- What kinds of significant learning do students engage in at school that are not a part of the mandated curriculum?
- As a group produce a nonlinguistic representation of our growing and increasingly interconnected understanding of how we learn.

Chapter Four

The Twenty-First Century Needs Us

We have spent some time looking at a few big fish. We have explored in depth the differences between the linear, print-based society and the influence it had on education. We also considered the changes being wrought by digital technology and different ways of thinking and of organizing society that have resulted. In the last chapter we also slowed down a while and looked more closely at what we mean by "learning" and by "education." We went beyond understanding the gist of it and looked in some detail and at some depth.

It's important that we do this because we need to understand what's happening, and it's hard to understand without taking time to focus and explore something in depth. It's what we need our children to do and it's what we need to do. If we can teach our children how to think effectively, efficiently, and creatively, then we will be giving them the most important skills with which to thrive within whatever the future may look like and have to offer them.

It is tempting to say, "I'm a busy person. Give me some down and dirty strategies I can use tomorrow." To follow that line would be for us to remain in the shallows, picking up one shiny idea after another. Things are changing fast, and the only way we can keep up with change is to focus and understand what is going on, to be nimble and quick thinking, and to work out our own strategies, ones that will suit your youngsters, your context, and the subject material you are working with.

THINKING NOT DROWNING: SURVIVING AND THRIVING IN THE TWENTY-FIRST CENTURY

A five-year-old entering school this year will finish year 12 in 2028. Given the speed of change it would be a very brave person who would be prepared to outline a body of knowledge that will be essential for a successful life in 2028.

What if it isn't about knowledge at all? Traditionally we have believed that there is a particular corpus of knowledge that every child should acquire. It varies from country to country and from state to state and we do know that if we put everything into the curriculum that various people think is essential, our children would still be in school when they are old and gray. We have also believed that there are certain routines that our youngsters should learn to do almost automatically. They should be fluent with a variety of mathematical and scientific formulae for example.

They should be able to put a set of values into the formula, crank the routine handle, and come up with the correct answer. How do you work out percentages? You apply a routine that requires you to put one number over another and multiply by 100. Generations of students have been taught this and remember it into adulthood—as a routine, often without understanding the routine and what it actually means.

There have been many attempts to clarify what we believe are the important kinds of learning needed to survive and thrive in this complex world and into the future. The United States National Academy of Sciences commissioned a report on "Defining deeper learning and 21st Century skills" (NRC, 2012).

The report found that these twenty-first-century skills fell into three categories: cognitive skills, interpersonal skills, and intrapersonal skills. There is no mention of the need to know any particular "stuff." Important historical dates, the periodic table, the life stages of the butterfly, the names of the oceans of the world—none of these are mentioned. This is not because they are unimportant or without merit.

Problems arise when we try to define essential knowledge in a world that changes so rapidly.

We need to look for something more fundamental and more enduring than facts and routines. In the twenty-first century our kids will need these skills:

Cognitive skills—the ability to carry out research, analyze, and think critically in various contexts—in books, online, through interviews, and the like.
Interpersonal skills—the ability to work cooperatively with others, resolve conflicts, listen actively, communicate clearly, plan and evaluate their own performance, and take on leadership.
Intrapersonal skills—to develop curiosity, initiative, self-direction, flexibility, and adaptability.

> We no longer simply need adults who can follow orders, read and write, and do basic mathematics. They were the skills for the Industrial Age and we are moving rapidly away from that. Sadly, when we look at what goes on in many schools it seems they haven't yet got the message.

Tony Wagner is the Innovation Education Fellow at the Technology & Entrepreneurship Center at Harvard University. In his book on the global achievement gap he points to the three fundamental transformations that have taken place in a very short period of time (Wagner, 2008):

- The rapid evolution of the new global "knowledge economy" and the ways in which the world of work—all work—is changing
- The sudden and dramatic shift from a world characterized by a limited amount and availability of information to world of information flux and glut
- The profound impact of media and technology on how young people learn, relate to the world, and to each other.

The Common Core State Standards have been designed to prepare students "to enter a world in which ... businesses are demanding more than ever before" (CCS, 2009).

What do business leaders judge to be the most valuable skills employees can bring to their jobs? Tony Wagner asked them and this is what they said:

- **Critical thinking and problem-solving**
  "The idea that a company's senior leaders have all the answers and can solve problems by themselves has gone completely by the wayside ...The person who's close to the work has to have strong analytic skills."—Ellen Kumata, consultant to Fortune 200 companies
- **Collaboration across networks and leading by influence**
  "The biggest problem we have in the company as a whole is finding people capable of exerting leadership across the board."—Mark Chandler, Senior Vice President and General Counsel at Cisco
- **Agility and adaptability**
  "I've been here four years, and we've done fundamental reorganization every year because of changes in the business ... I can guarantee the job I hire someone to do will change or may not exist in the future."—Clay Parker, President of Chemical Management Division of BOC Edwards
- **Initiative and entrepreneurship**
  "For our production and crafts staff, the hourly workers, we need self-directed people ... who can find creative solutions to some very tough, challenging problems."—Mark Maddox, Human Resources Manager at Unilever Foods North America
- **Effective oral and written communication**
  "The biggest skill people are missing is the ability to communicate: both written and oral presentations."—Annmarie Neal, Vice President for Talent Management at Cisco Systems

- **Accessing and analyzing information**
  "There is so much information available that it is almost too much, and if people aren't prepared to process the information effectively, it almost freezes them in their steps."—Mike Summers, Vice President for Global Talent Management at Dell
- **Curiosity and imagination**
  "Our old idea is that work is defined by employers and that employees have to do whatever the employer wants…but actually, you would like him to come up with an interpretation that you like—he's adding something personal—a creative element."—Michael Jung, Senior Consultant at McKinsey and Company

These skills represent the real needs of business at all levels. They are also the skills needed to be a good citizen and to lead a happy and productive life. Each of these business leaders is asking for the same thing—creative, flexible deep thinkers.

Mike Summers points directly to the problem to which we are devoting much of this book—the overabundance of information. In common with each of the others he wants employees who can effectively process and not be overwhelmed or distracted by this abundance.

They are all looking for people who can think in the deep end.

Parents and teachers who help children understand what these skills entail and how to continuously improve them empower children for successful lives. Too often these are not the primary skills taught in our schools. Nor are they the things we test to determine how effective our schools are being in preparing our youngsters for the world.

KEY IDEAS IN THIS CHAPTER

- To survive and thrive in the twenty-first century our children need to develop very different skills from those suited to the nineteenth and twentieth centuries.
- Curriculum focus needs to be firmly on developing skills that are fundamentally about effective, efficient, flexible, and creative thinking.
- In particular we need to be teaching cognitive, interpersonal, and intrapersonal skills and not simply facts and automatic routines.
- If we ask the business community what they need we find overwhelming support for this view.

DISCUSSION

- How much of the curriculum content you teach, or your child is taught, is devoted to factual information and the teaching of routines?
- To what extent are these twenty-first-century skills embedded in your curriculum? Share some examples.
- Do the classroom management processes utilized with your students have their foundations in Skinner's behaviorism, in obedience to authority or something else?
- How do you help your students to develop interpersonal skills? Do you find a need to focus on some of these skills more than others?
- What strategies do you use to encourage your students to be reflective and to self-regulate their learning?
- Consider a recent teaching unit. How many sources did your students use to obtain information? What guidelines did they have to evaluate the quality of their research findings?
- What specific examples can you find within your school of students learning from each other in preference to learning from the adults in the school?
- Do you see dangers inherent in students learning from one another? What benefits you can make use of in your teaching?
- If you would like to explore these twenty-first-century skills in a little more detail, you will find the table below helpful. It analyzes the cognitive, interpersonal, and intrapersonal skills more closely.

Chapter Five

What Is Happening in Our Schools?

Given all of this growing pool of knowledge, what are we seeing in our schools today?

Do the practices commonly in use reflect our growing understandings about how people learn?

Are we equipping our youngsters to be effective, deep thinkers in the digital world?

Sadly, a review of what goes on in many public schools today reveals that not much has changed since the days of the Industrial Revolution. We are still focused on literacy and numeracy, we reward students for doing as they are told, for achieving standardized goals that are set by others, and for following educational tracks that have, in the past, turned them into productive members of the work force for the Industrial Age, but which will not be adequate for the increasingly digital Information Age.

"College and Career Ready." What is that?

In the introduction to Common Core State Standards information about "What Parents Should Know" (CCS, 2009), we read:

> To ensure all students are ready for success after high school, the Common Core State Standards establish clear, consistent guidelines for what every student should know and be able to do in math and English language arts from kindergarten through 12th grade.

Good luck with that. Given the rapid pace of change, for what kinds of careers are we preparing them? What will be the content of college courses look like in 2029?

Common Core doesn't close its eyes to this conundrum. A little further on in the same document it recognizes there is something else:

> The Common Core focuses on developing the critical-thinking, problem-solving, and analytical skills students will need to be successful.

We should be preparing them to be inquisitive, thoughtful, and creative thinkers able to take their place as informed, efficacious members of a democratic society.

Looking at the future through the rear view mirror,

> We look at the present through a rear view mirror. We march backwards into the future. (McLuhan and Fiore, 2001)

Why is it that so many of our schools continue to be run as if they were nineteenth-century factories? Some schools are incorporating a much deeper understanding of how children learn into their teaching strategies and their organizational frameworks, but many still seem to view learning within the behaviorist model, where the emphasis is on rewards and punishments. Often these rewards are subtle and revolve around Maslow's notions about the need for self-esteem. We praise the students according to the test scores they receive and we use the negative reinforcement of a failure in an assignment in the hope that this will help extinguish less desirable school and study behaviors.

In these backwards-looking schools and school systems, the focus is firmly on standardization and measurement. Students are processed in batches based on nothing more than birth date and we hear a lot of talk about "value-added" assessments as if our children are raw material to be processed in some kind of assembly line.

IS YOUR CLASSROOM A FACTORY?

Does your classroom resemble an assembly line? Are the children seated neatly in rows? Do they spend a lot of time all doing the same task? Is every child measured against the same yard stick? Is your daily schedule unchangeable?

What would you do if your lesson plan says this afternoon we are doing geography and thinking about the oceans of the world, but a child arrives in the classroom after lunch play breathless with excitement and with a live, wriggling worm in his hand?

I recall a teacher of six-year-olds in exactly this predicament. She realized that deeper learning was possible when the children had the opportunity to focus on one thing that had grasped their attention already. She understood the importance of knowing a lot about one thing, something important to the children at the time, rather than knowing a little about a lot of things that had little importance to them.

She abandoned her lesson plan and spent the afternoon on worms. She sent a child to the library to ask the librarian for all the worm books she could find. The children spent time on close observation of the worm and the teacher shared what knowledge she had with them. A list was made on the board of all the things they knew about worms and key words were circled. These became the day's spelling words.

She then asked them to think more deeply, to take a different view of the world and imagine how things might look if you were a worm. The children went into the yard and lay on their bellies before returning to their seats and drawing pictures of the world from a worm's eye point of view. The teacher then asked the children to do something when they went home that night—find out one interesting thing about worms.

The next morning the children shared the things they had found out overnight. The teacher had found a worm poem, which she had written on a large sheet of chart paper. The teacher read the poem to the children and then they joined in. The reading lesson that morning included the worm poem. The teacher covered up all the nouns with blank pieces of paper. The children read the poem again, predicting the nouns they could no longer see. She then did the same thing with the verbs and then with the small connecting words.

Of course, the ability to do this requires a teacher who is skilled in flexible thinking. Too many of our schools have resorted to various forms of scripted and programmed learning where the teacher has become little more than a facilitator, following a script or methodology designed by someone else and for an imaginary group of students who may have very little in common with the class for which that teacher has responsibility.

Do you see aspects of your classroom, school, or school district in this? Some schools and school systems seem to do their best to standardize the inputs in the only way they know how, or that is practically feasible—by original date of manufacture (birth date). They then develop processing techniques (curriculum and teaching strategies) and try hard to standardize these across every factory (school). These are the curricula and teaching practices that are required in order for the process workers (teachers), to get positive evaluations.

Cheaply administered tests are designed to ensure that every end product (child) meets the same criteria of successful processing (schooling). At the end of each processing year every module (child) submits to the same test, or quality assurance measure, to determine the extent of the value added to the raw material. Faulty modules (children) who do not meet the standard are reprocessed, through either the repetition of the previous processing system (by repeating the school year) or some form of modified processing (remedial classes), until they do meet the standard.

In the industrial age the core of the assembly line factory was standardized measurement of quality. This is a fine criterion if you intend to produce high-quality identical widgets, but it is neither effective nor appropriate if you intend to develop a diverse "think force" for the twenty-first century. It is precisely this practice permeating too much of current education systems that risks destroying quality education and ensuring that our children will fail in the twenty-first century.

Why? Because our children are not widgets and learning, as we have seen, does not work like that. Over decades we have come to understand what a rich and complex process learning actually is. We need to ensure that ALL our schools reflect both this complex and growing understanding of learning as well as an appreciation of the massive changes that the digital age has brought to the needs of society.

Real, transformational learning requires interested students. It takes place when they are fascinated by something, when they develop a passion for a subject. Ken Robinson is a visionary and widely respected cultural and educational leader and he has explored this eloquently in a number of TED talks and in his books (Robinson, 2011, 2013).

DIVERSITY RULES

It has become commonplace to talk about "individual differences," but do our interactions with youngsters really reflect a deep understanding of this concept? Our strength as a species comes from our diversity not our uniformity. The digital age is placing the opportunity for diversity at our finger tips, because it provides an almost limitless pool of information and interconnectedness within easy reach of anyone with a smart device—a computer, a tablet, and a smartphone.

Every child has the capacity to be fascinated by something different but schools, with their standardized curricula and testing, run the risk of stifling this diversity in order to ensure that every child learns exactly the same thing. The development of a variety of national curricula occupies the minds of educators in different parts of the world as they try to decide what everyone needs to learn.

One of the key indicators of the inadequacy of our current system of education is the number of individuals who achieve outstanding success in spite of it. Look at the school dropouts who have been successful mainly through their passion for subjects not taught in schools. Many of these completed their compulsory education, entered college to clarify and extend their passion, and then took a risk by leaving the standard track and going off on their own. Others left long before reaching tertiary education.

The following people, all dropouts, are important contributors to this digital age and its Information Revolution. The dollar values associated with their net worth or company value are included only to indicate the material extent of their accomplishments, not because money by itself is a measure of success.

Paul Allen and Bill Gates dropped out of the University of Washington to found Microsoft. Together they are worth $70 billion.

Steve Jobs dropped out of Reed College and joined up with University of California dropout Steve Wozniak to form Apple Computers in 1976. Apple is now worth about $500 billion.

Larry Ellison dropped out of the University of Illinois and then the University of Chicago to eventually form Oracle. Ellison is worth $36 billion.

Michael Dell dropped out of the University of Texas Medical School to form Dell Computer in 1984. Michael Dell is worth over $16 billion.

Mark Zukerberg dropped out of Harvard University to begin Facebook in 2004 and he could be worth up to $28 billion.

Jack Dorsey dropped out of New York University to form Twitter in 2008 and his net worth is already estimated at $650 million.

Sir Alan Sugar dropped out of school in London at the age of sixteen. He went on to develop Britain's first mass produced home computer— Amstrad—and is today worth more than $1.5 billion.

James Cameron, a Canadian, switched from physics to English at Fullerton College before dropping out entirely. He went on to become one of the world's foremost movie directors, nominated for six Academy Awards and estimated to have earned in 2010 alone around $257 million.

Richard Branson has dyslexia and demonstrated consistently poor academic performance before dropping out of school at sixteen. He went on to found a slew of Virgin branded companies and is currently around the fourth richest citizen of the United Kingdom.

Consider these names: Ted Turner, David Plouffe (advisor to President Obama), Ellen Degeneris, Tiger Woods, Brad Pitt, Toni Collette, Madonna, Oprah Winfrey, Ralph Lauren, John Lennon ... and so the list goes on.

Dropping out of school is not a key to success. We know how much harder it is for a young person without at least a high school diploma to find satisfactory employment. The tragedy is that these brilliant people all seemed to find school frustrating, boring, or irrelevant. They were prepared to launch themselves, to take risks, and then to succeed in spite of their education. As

Malcolm Gladwell has explained in his book *Outliers*, much of their subsequent success had to do with being at the right place at the right time. Not all school dropouts have such lucky breaks.

What will become of all the other young people who find school irrelevant or boring but who do not have the lucky breaks or the circumstances that enable them to take risks? And perhaps just as importantly, what are our schools losing when the best and brightest leave them?

We learn best when we take risks, when we chance failure, because even though it is really difficult material, it fascinates us enough to make the risks and the hard work worthwhile.

Seth Godin, in his October 2012 TEDx Youth talk "Stop Stealing Dreams," uses a powerful analogy (Goodin, 2012). Godin says that we are focused on getting our students to collect facts or "dots" and we measure success by how many dots they have accumulated by the end of the school year. Instead, we should be teaching them to connect the dots, and this we are too often failing to do.

Thinking is all about understanding and connecting the dots. Google has made the belief that there is some set of facts that is somehow mandatory learning for every student an archaic notion. The Internet means that we are constantly swimming in a sea of information. We have a glut of information. A simple web search can provide you with information about almost anything you can imagine. In this vast array of bits of information, what is most important, what is trustworthy?

That is a straightforward question, with no easy answer. It all depends—on who you are, where you are, what you are doing, what you need, what you want, and what you intend to do next. With so much information available to us, what we need most is an effective set of filters. We need to be able to filter out the information that is not relevant, not reliable, and not helpful.

Instead of arguing about what information should and should not be included in any school curriculum, we should be focused on how we help young people develop these filters.

We need to teach them how to think. You cannot think without something to think about, but one of the fundamental criteria by which we should judge the content of any curriculum is this—how does it *advance* the students' ability to think? The real issues are not which events in history should be included in year 9, or whether it is more important that they read Steinbeck or Hemingway. We can argue, and curriculum developers often do, about the most appropriate time to teach cell division, the water cycle, or the migration patterns of birds. What is most important is how the content we eventually decide upon can contribute to the development of skillful thinkers.

~ I recall observing a lesson where the children were learning about the burning of Washington by the British in 1814. It would have been easy to send the students off to independently research what had happened and why it happened. Instead she chose to provide an opportunity for the children to think in more depth about just one aspect of the event. This teacher was much more interested in having her students *understand* what happened rather than simply *remember* what happened.

She was a good teacher and she understood that children are far more likely to understand something if they can relate it to their own lives, and so she asked them this question, "If you had to flee your home because of fire, what is the one most important thing you would take with you?" She gave the children time to think about this and to share their thoughts with each other in small groups. When the class came together the children explained their choices to one another. The teacher made a list on the board of the reasons different children gave for their choices: it would be useful, my mother gave it to me, I would be afraid and this makes me feel safer, my dad would be angry if I lost it, it cost a lot of money, it's the only photo of grandad we have, and so on.

After exploring their own thoughts the teacher revealed to the students that Dolly Madison had saved a portrait of George Washington. From this deeper understanding about what makes things important to individuals they were able to discuss why Dolly Madison had chosen to save a portrait rather than the family jewels or silver ware. By focusing in depth on one thing, they had come to an understanding of an historical event within a human context. They didn't just remember, they understood.

WHO ARE THE EDUCATORS TODAY?

Education isn't just what goes on at school. Everyone who comes in contact with a child is educating that child. Parents and teachers are obviously among the primary educators of our children, but so are shopkeepers, police, baby sitters, politicians, flight attendants, taxi drivers and bus drivers, school crossing guards, and the people who read our water and electricity meters. If you come into contact with a child, if a child sees you interacting with your environment or other people, then you are a participant in the act of educating that child. When we educate our children we teach them about the values in our society, we help them learn how to function effectively within that society, and how to make the most of themselves.

~ Every trip to the supermarket can be an opportunity to slow down and begin to take a close look at what is going on, to understand what is happening.

Scanning the shelves and seeing the exchange of money for goods tells the child a lot about the practicalities of living in his community. Watching another parent dealing harshly with a rambunctious child helps develop an understanding about the varieties of people in society and the fact that some live very different lives, with very different values. The way the school crossing guard deals with children helps them understand that our society has structures in place to protect us and keep us safe. Each of these experiences offers an opportunity to disengage from the experience itself and think about what was happening.

We can help our kids to move from simply being participants in and observers of experiences. That's the realm of the shallows. By helping to think about their experiences and observations we help them move into deeper water.

In the classroom and at home we organize our physical environments. We put things away in certain places for good reasons. Our cutlery is placed in a divided tray, our socks in the same dresser drawer, and the classroom books are not simply placed haphazardly around the classroom. Children observe this every day, but do we give them opportunities to think about why we do this, and why we organize the ways in which we do? "Don't just do something, stand there" as Art Costa once said.

Think about your world, go a little deeper and ask why, escape from the shallow water of simple observations and fleeting experiences. Stop and think. Flexible and creative thinking can then be encouraged by asking children to develop new ideas about how we might organize some aspect of our environments.

When he visits his grandparents the child learns that sometimes we treat different generations differently, we behave differently, and we use different language. Hopefully he will come to understand why this is so, that different life experiences create different expectations, that societies change over time, and that what might be appropriate in one setting may be very inappropriate in another.

Children can explore these differences by explicitly comparing the language choices they make when hanging out with their friends after school and when going to visit grandparents. Older children might look at the different subjects appropriate in each context, about the different vocabulary, or the sentence structure. We can allow our youngsters to let these human interactions simply flow over and around them, or we can take the time to help them slow down, focus, and think about what is happening.

Simple questions in passing can lead to deeper thinking and understanding: Why do you think they have self-service checkouts in supermarkets? What do you think it would be like to have six brothers and sisters? How would you feel if you were an only child? What do you think you have to do if you are a crossing guard at a school? Do they have crossing guards at universities? After a shopping trip where you witnessed a mother smacking her child you might ask your children what they thought about it, how the mother was feeling, and how the child felt.

There are so many circumstances when we can help our children to become better thinkers, better able to look at the world in all its complexity, and work out the patterns and understand why things are as they are. To think below the surface.

We all have a responsibility in this, not just teachers. The thing about clichés is that they often become clichés because there is something deeply true about them. "It takes a village to raise a child" is one such cliché. Children learn from every experience and we can all help to ensure that those experiences lead children to think more deeply about their world.

Society has come to regard schools as the places where most of the important learning takes place. We need to change that. We can help parents and other community members understand that while schools can be a hub for learning, we are all in the task together. By ensuring that children see schools as a part of the community and not divorced from it, they will also come to see that what goes on in the school is of relevance to what goes in life. Thinking doesn't just happen at school, and good thinking should happen all the time.

Recall the words attributed to Socrates: they were powerful two thousand five hundred years ago and they continue to be powerful today. "I cannot teach anybody anything. I can only teach them to think."

KEY IDEAS IN THIS CHAPTER

- Given the speed of change in society it is virtually impossible to specify what body of knowledge our youngsters will need when they leave school.
- If we want them to be "college and career ready" we need to be focused on developing the twenty-first-century skills of effective, analytical, creative, flexible thinking—deep thinking.
- Many of our schools are still tied to the educational outcomes that best suited the industrial age—obedience, literacy, and numeracy.
- Standardized curricula and testing tend to lead to conformity when we know that our strengths as a society come from our diversity. This is why some of our most creative and successful adults were unsuccessful at school.

- The skill that will last whatever the future looks like is the ability to think.
- By slowing down and looking into the deeper water, asking the deeper questions, we can all be educators whether we are professional teachers or not.

DISCUSSION

- Describe a situation you have experienced in school recently where you created an opportunity for creative thinking that went beyond the information that was available.
- What everyday tasks do you think would be worth thinking about in greater depth?
- What is your school currently doing to connect with the community about significant things to do with learning and not just about fundraising?
- Who could you bring into the conversation in your school other than parents?
- Can you identify a student in your school/class who has a passion for something? Are you able to make use of that passion to further his/her learning?
- If you look carefully at a day of teaching in your classroom, how much time is spent collecting dots and how much time is spent connecting dots?

Chapter Six

The Digital Divides

Immigrants and Natives, Real and Virtual

To people of the "old world," the linear world, the pace, and complexity of life today seem overwhelming. For those who were born before the interconnectedness of the Internet, the cell phone, and social media, the people Marc Prensky calls "digital immigrants," there is a constant struggle to keep up with a new culture, new codes of behavior, and a new language, just as there is for any geographical immigrant.

But nothing about this new world is frightening for the "digital natives"—the young people who have never known a world without interconnectedness. To them the electronic digital age is simply how it is and how it has always been for them. They are comfortable in this web of communication, and they have never been more connected.

WE CAN LOOK AT THE "DIGITAL DIVIDE" IN TWO DIFFERENT WAYS

First, there is the divide between the digital natives—kids who have grown up in the digital age, and the digital immigrants—newcomers to this nonlinear, fast, and furious world of interconnections and information overload. We need the adults, the teachers, and the parents to inhabit the digital world as fully as they can so that they can guide the children as they explore and become more and familiar with the digital world and its advantages as well as its dangers.

There is a second divide that we also explore—the divide between the physical, here and now world, and the digital, virtual world. It is important that we recognize this divide because our young people run the risk of losing touch with the intricacies and subtleties of life in the physical world because of their attachment to the beguiling digital world. They are so intimately and constantly connected to the virtual, digital world that they sometimes see it as a replacement for the physical world. Lovers think an SMS is an acceptable way of ending a relationship, people watch exciting, live events through the view finders of their mobile phones, and complex messages are reduced to 140 characters on Twitter. We examine this divide in more detail in the next chapter.

LIFE AND THE BRAIN DON'T WORK IN STRAIGHT LINES

Perhaps one of the reasons why digital media are so captivating is because they so closely resemble the workings of the human brain. Young people who have grown up within this environment feel totally at home. In the past, if we tried to find a metaphor for the brain, we might have come up with something like a library, or perhaps a library inside a factory. It seemed that in our brains we stored all the bits and pieces we had learned in our lives in some kind of neurological filing system. Everything was tidily in its place and we could pretty reliably assume that one part of the brain dealt with language, another with mathematics, another with emotions, and so on.

We were applying a linear model, an industrial model to the operations of the brain. We also thought that we could measure with considerable accuracy the effectiveness of the processes of thinking by the use of various intelligence tests. Applicants for the military, teaching, and many other forms of training were first given intelligence tests to ensure the quality of the raw materials before processing began.

With the advent of functional magnetic resonance imaging we are discovering how simplistic and in many ways downright wrong this view was. We are now able to examine and see people thinking, to map the areas of brain that are active when a person is solving an addition problem, watching a sad movie, or struggling to regain speech after a stroke. In the human brain there are approximately one hundred billion nerve cells or neurons and each makes between a thousand and ten thousand connections with other neurons and each connection can be either on or off.

V M Ramachandran, in his book *The Tell-Tale Brain*, tells us that "With all these permutations the number of possible brain states is staggeringly vast; in fact it easily exceeds the number of elementary particles in the known universe." Add to this complexity the fact that the connections, once formed, are not static. They continually change and this change is called neuroplasticity. The brain is plastic; the brain you had when you began to read this book is not the same as the brain you have now.

This network of ever-changing connections and interactions is startlingly similar to the network of the World Wide Web. We might not be too far off the mark if we saw the Internet as a simpler analog of the human brain. Could this be one of the reasons why our young people, who have grown up with this network as a familiar part of their lives, feel so at home enmeshed within it?

THE BRAIN IS A NETWORK OPERATING WITHIN A NETWORKED WORLD

Here is where it gets more conjectural, but also very interesting. The Internet has stored within it a vast amount of information in the form of books, pictures, music, and words—a bit like a massive library. It also contains programs that can manipulate this content and create new things—a bit like a factory. But it is also connected internally to different bits of itself and a huge external network spanning the entire globe. Overnight, there are things that appear there that were not there when you went to sleep.

The Internet updates itself constantly, people have left messages, and Facebook, Twitter, and a myriad other social media sites, web pages, and digital newspapers all have different content and they all change from second to second, with new information, events, and commentaries as the day progresses. The Internet is plastic, rather like your brain. It is entirely possible that in the future it will become just as complex as our brains, but we are not there yet.

By utilizing the computing power of the cloud and by basing its software algorithms on the neural network model of the brain, sophisticated artificial intelligence is just around the corner.

YOUR KIDS' BRAINS ARE NOT LIKE YOURS

Everyone's brain will develop a little differently and there will be vast commonalities, but the fine-tuning of the brain is an interactive process between biology and experience. The world our youngsters are experiencing is increasingly different from the world of the previous generation. Their brains reflect this difference.

Young people sense the inappropriateness of the linear, specialized, differentiated world of their parents and grandparents, the world in which a good education today meant a good job tomorrow and security for life. They know that in a dynamic, plastic, and interconnected world things are just not as predictable as that. Night might follow day, and 3 might follow 2, but school is not necessarily followed by employment and there is no one set of marketable skills and no corpus of information that will guarantee the future.

It has become a cliché to say that the jobs children entering school today will be doing when they leave haven't been invented yet.

And so what one thing do we know without doubt that they will need to be able to do, in this shifting, plastic, dynamic future that will be upon them with the inevitability of death and taxes?

They need to be able to think effectively.

CHILDHOOD, VALUES, AND DOING AS YOU ARE TOLD

Childhood is an invention of the last four hundred years or so. The notion of an intermediate stage between childhood and adulthood is very new, and with it have come a slew of protections designed to safeguard the immature person from the predations of the world, as well as to provide a space within which values can become firmly rooted and a path through the world can begin to be forged.

HOW DID WE LEARN OUR VALUES AND PLACE IN THE WORLD?

Until very recently children learned values and their roles in society through the family. By watching the parents and their interactions with their community, and by the disciplining and direct instruction of family, church, school, and community, our children learned appropriate behaviors and moral, family values. The culture, and all that implies, was passed down from one generation to the next, so that a child's behavior and attitudes could be expected to be a reflection of the values of their parents. It was a largely vertical, linear process, from one generation to the next.

For this to work, children needed to be obedient, to do as they were told. Corporal punishment was meted out to deal with infractions of the rules in the same way as the community or the state meted out punishments to those who broke the rules and laws of society. Children and adolescents were expected to pay attention to adults and to learn from them.

Only a few children would grow up to be bosses. Most would work at a relatively low level in the hierarchical chain of command. Even if they were promoted to a higher position, it would still involve submission to the directives of those more senior. The entire commercial, industrial, and bureaucratic apparatus depended on an orderly agreed system of obedience, of doing as one was told.

HOW DO OUR KIDS LEARN THEIR VALUES AND PLACE IN THE WORLD?

The arrival of television was an instrumental player because for the first time youngsters were able to watch others of their own age, see how they lived in distant parts of the world, and compare their values and aspirations with their own. Teenagers became aware of themselves as a distinct entity in society. They watched each other.

In their own living rooms, young people saw the intimacy of other families' dinner table conversations, their arguments, their joys, and their choices in clothes and music. From *Leave It to Beaver* to *Welcome Back, Kotter* the television age gave adolescents glimpses of lives that challenged their own, which pushed and pulled at the values and attitudes being handed down by their parents. Teenage rebellion was fueled by these images as young people began to question.

The vertical transmission of values within the family unit was being replaced by the horizontal network of mass communication as young people began to experience themselves as a social layer rather than isolated kids whose closest ties were within the family. Facebook, Twitter, and the ever-present cell phone connect our young people, sometimes more firmly to one another than to the older generation.

WHERE DO THE GROWN-UPS FIT IN?

Until we know what our kids are hearing and seeing we will have no way to be a positive influence on their development of values. We cannot just leave them to get on with it.

The network is hugely influential and it tugs and pulls in multiple directions. If our young people feel confused and lacking clear directions we should not feel surprised. It is often the case that they have not been able to find the space to think more deeply. They have not been able to disentangle themselves from the network for long enough to consider it thoughtfully. They have not been able to move out of the stimulation, variety, and fascination of the shallows and into the quieter, more contemplative deeper waters where they can slow down, focus, and think deeply.

THE GROWN-UPS HAVE IMPORTANT THINGS TO SHARE

Immigrants always need to learn the culture, adapt, and integrate. But we mustn't lose sight of the fact that every immigrant adds something of value to their new culture. They bring with them their own ways of thinking and behaving. Our generation may well be the digital immigrants, working hard to assimilate into the digital world but we have much that is valuable to teach our children.

Specialization, focus, linear thinking, and problem-solving were the skills that got us to where we are now. They created the digital era. While welcoming the new, networked, nonlinear world of the electronic age, we must not lose those skills. It's not a case of either/or, but it's a case of holding on to the best of the past while embracing the gifts and opportunities of the new.

We can only share if we can become part of the conversations our youngsters have. Getting into the conversation doesn't mean sitting in on our kids' online conversations or following them around during the school day, listening over their shoulders. It means creating, over time, an atmosphere where they will share with us their own thinking as they sort out the world around them.

If we want young people to share the contents of their minds with us, we will need to learn how to suspend judgment. It is almost impossible to form a productive relationship with someone when they feel they are being judged. We want to be able to guide our youngsters to think about their own thinking. We want them to become habitual deep divers.

The values they are observing and hearing about them as they explore their interactive world may well be very different from ours. Some of them may be dangerous, and some may have the potential to open our minds a little more broadly. We may be shocked, and we may be amused. We need to keep our reactions to ourselves!

WHAT DOES THIS LOOK LIKE IN PRACTICE?

When a student in your class tells you that we should not let immigrants into our country because they are different from us and won't fit in, what is the best response?

You might say that there are laws and regulations that allow a certain number of immigrants every year, that prejudice is antisocial, and that we have benefited over the years from the inclusion of people from different racial and cultural backgrounds. You might encourage the class to examine some documents outlining immigration policies over the years, to read some articles, and to listen to a visiting speaking from a different cultural background.

The student may or may not choose to listen, or to accept what you are handing him. Remember, youngsters are less inclined to simply accept the views of those in authority. They want to be a part of the process.

🌊 On the other hand, you can make him a part of the process, and you can guide him to explore his own thinking, to interrogate it, and to test it. You can encourage him to think in the deep end by focusing on his thoughts and thinking below the surface. And the first thing he will need to will be to fully and accurately verbalize his thoughts.

One of the sixteen habits of mind articulated by Costa and Kallick is "thinking and communicating with clarity and precision" (Costa and Kallick, 2008). When we put thoughts into words we are engaged in a continuing process of pinning our ideas down. When we invite a student to tell us his opinion about something, we start him off on a process of exploration, and we begin to take him into the deep end of thinking.

Initially his opinions will have been the result of his exposure to a vast range of sources and experiences—things he has heard from his peers and from adults, things he has read or watched on television, advertisements, and interactions between people that he has observed—the list could go on and on. All of these surface impressions have coalesced into an opinion.

Our task is to get that young person to think more deeply about those impressions. We need to help him disentangle himself from the web of impressions by focusing on just one or two.

A useful first step might be to brainstorm with the class where opinions about immigration have come from. Keep a record on the white board so that a visual impression of the breadth of these sources becomes apparent. As is always the case with brainstorming, this is a judgment-free zone. Every contribution is accepted without comment.

You might need to push their thinking in order to get as complete a picture as possible. The goal here is to capture the full complexity, variety, and vibrancy of experiences that help to form our opinions. Don't be afraid to spend a bit of time on this step. You are laying the foundation for what comes next.

Now you will want to guide your students to think more deeply about just one or two of these sources, to disentangle from the surface and dive deeper, focusing on a narrower spectrum.

Tread gently. Your goal is not to be another addition to the profusion of impressions that bumped up against each other on the surface, in the shallow water.

STOP TELLING, START ASKING: THE POWER OF GOOD QUESTIONS

Some words, such as *how* and *why*, can act like the weights on a diver's belt, enabling her to escape from the surface and head for the depths. Let the kids in on the secret. Tell them what you are helping them to do. Encourage them to come up with their own questions to interrogate the surface ideas. Help them to use language that is increasingly precise.

~ The example that follows can be readily adapted to a discussion between a parent and a child. It's not only about teachers and students.

> *Student:* "Older people don't like my generation."
> *Teacher:* "That's an interesting point of view. Who agrees? Tell us how you came to that conclusion."

LIST ON WHITE BOARD

- My parents get mad with me all the time.
- Everyone knows about the generation gap.
- They don't approve of how we dress.
- They listen to weird music.
- They think our music is weird.
- They tell us we'll all get good jobs if we stay at school.
- My parents are narrow minded when we have discussions.
- I can't tell my parents stuff, they just get mad/ tell me I'm wrong/get upset.
- The expressions on older people's faces when I'm with a group of friends at the mall.
- I keep reading about the generation gap in newspapers.
- I watch ... on TV and the kids are always fighting with their parents.

And the list goes on until there is no more to add.

> *Teacher:* "OK. We've collected a lot of impressions. Let's do some thinking in greater depth. Which one of these impressions shall we look at more closely? Remember we are going to use language that is as precise as possible, so I'll give you plenty of time to choose your words."

Remember that the objective here is to get these young people to think more deeply about the horizontal transmission of values, and so it is very important that they listen to one another rather than listening just to the teacher. As we pointed out earlier, opinions often grow as the result of a multitude of surface impressions, glimpses that individually may not mean too much, but together form a powerful influence on our behavior and opinions. We absorb these impressions without ever examining any of them in any depth.

These youngsters are enmeshed in their own culture and in the world of mass and social media. Our goal is to help them focus and think deeply about the messages they are receiving from one another and from that world of mass and social media, and to express their thoughts with clarity and precision.

Perhaps they will select to think more deeply about the impression that their parents are "mad" with them a lot of the time. Since we have been thinking particularly about the concept of "obedience" you might use that as an opportunity to encourage the students to think more deeply about how we all learn how to behave and what might be leading to their parents' frustration. It is now that they begin to pay attention to words such as "why" and "how."

Youngsters often have difficulty in seeing the world from another's view point. The ability to do this grows with maturity and with practice and is the root of empathy. This could be a useful time to help your students put themselves in someone else's shoes as they try to untangle what it is that causes their parents to react as they do to their adolescent behavior, at the same time as they learn to think more deeply and in a more focused manner.

Some useful questions might be

- How do your parents show that they are mad with you?
- The word "mad" isn't very precise. Is there a way you could describe your parents' behavior that would help me to understand it?
- How do you feel when they are like this? Is it a pleasant time for anyone?
- What sorts of things set them off? Can you see anything in common with these triggers?
- How could you predict when your parents are likely to get mad with you?
- Think of some ways that you might forestall them that would leave you both feeling better.

> We cannot stress too heavily how important it is to stop telling and start asking. The goal is to get these youngsters to think about their own thinking. We want them to interrogate their own thoughts and opinions. We don't simply want to provide them with an alternative set that we you have developed.

The same process can be carried out with much younger children. The language and the questions may be different but the process will be the same.

KEY IDEAS IN THIS CHAPTER

- The digital divide can exist in two different ways:
  - The digital natives and the digital immigrants
  - The real, physical world and the digital, virtual world.

- Perhaps digital natives are at ease within the networked digital world because it is so similar to the way the brain works. The brain is a complex network too and both are continually changing.
- We may not be able to predict what tomorrow will look like but we can predict that we will need to be good thinkers.
- In the past values and attitudes were passed down from generation to generation. Because of their immersion in the digital world and the rich horizontal communication among young people, many of their values and attitudes are learned from one another.
- Grown-up digital immigrants have important things to share because linear ways of thinking are still very important. It's our task to ensure these skills are taught.
- We need to stop telling and start asking so that youngsters feel a part of the process and not just the recipients of the older generation's wisdom.
- The wise use of questioning can lead youngsters to develop more focus and to dig below the surface of their initial thoughts.

DISCUSSION

- What aspects of the wider digital world make you feel uncomfortable?
- Identify what it is about these aspects that creates this sense of discomfort.
- Create a graphic representation of the way a person in the predigital or literate culture would view their life progression. Do the same for a digital native.
- Describe some of the problems you see arising from kids today learning values and attitudes from one another.
- How do you share your knowledge and experience with the youngsters with whom you interact. Does it work?
- What are some of the characteristics of questions that encourage deeper thought. What is it that makes one question so much better than another at encouraging deeper, more focused thinking?

Chapter Seven

Contrary to Popular Opinion, Television Can Help Bridge the Divide

We touched briefly in the previous chapter on the role of television to influence the values and attitudes of youngsters. It can also provide another context for interaction between the generations and open up opportunities for deeper thinking.

Television has been blamed by many commentators for ending conversation within the family. We imagine the family seated in a semicircle around the screen and the only verbal interactions are telling one another to be quiet. Perhaps even more worrying is the tendency for everyone to have their own television set in their own bedroom

> But television has the power to bring us together as much as to separate us.

In preliterate times members of the community would sit around the fire and share stories. There was a level of intimacy and interaction as different individuals and different generations responded each in their own ways. Children might ask questions of their elders and during the day individuals and groups might reflect upon the stories of the previous evening.

Literacy brought with it the era of private reading. In the living rooms of the educated, literate members of the community might spend their evenings in conversation, but increasingly they would be spent reading. When we read we don't always like to be interrupted and we each read our own separate book. One of the gifts of the book is its ability to immerse us in a different world, distinct from the physical world that surrounds us at the time.

It might be a world of the imagination with fictitious characters experiencing familiar dilemmas or perhaps fantastic characters facing problems entirely outside the range of our experience. The world might be one of thought, an investigation into an area of knowledge or the attempts of others to solve real-world problems. The possibilities are endless.

The important thing, however, is that in the literate living room each person is in their own world of the book, independent of others in the physical room. Reading in this sense isolates us from one another.

Television offers an experience very different from reading and more similar to the preliterate experiences around the camp fire. If we have not succumbed to the temptation of putting a television in every room of the house (and in particular, in each of the children's bedrooms), we can find ourselves sitting sharing the same stories, commenting to each other about the puzzles, the emotions, the discoveries, and the twists and turns of plots.

We still read books and appreciate the precious qualities of isolation from the frenzied world, the opportunities to go deeply into a carefully defined world of story or information free from distractions. But with an electronic medium such as television we have the opportunity once again to experience things as members of a networked, interactive family both within and outside the home, and television can also be a place for deeper thought.

WHERE IS TELEVISION IN THE COMMON CORE?

The Common Core State Standards explore the use of electronic media in the Speaking and Listening component of the English Language Arts Standards. The focus, however, is firmly on the use of these media for the "Presentation of Knowledge and Ideas." The study of literature is similarly focused on written texts although in grades 7 and 8 there is an opportunity to look more closely at the visual interpretation in film of a written text. True, there is specific reference to the consideration of drama as written text, stage presentation, and its depiction on film, but television is conspicuous by its absence as a serious focus of study.

That's a pity. The television screen can become a kind of fireplace, nurturing conversation through shared experiences. The following morning at work we often find people chatting about last night's plot developments in a popular drama series or discussing the arguments and insights gained from watching an interview or a news report.

📖 A focused discussion on plot development can be founded on a popular television drama. Watching at home, youngsters could then graphically outline the plot lines and the interactions between the different characters. Not every student needs to have watched the same series or program. If they have based their graphic representations of plot on different programs, this provides opportunities to compare and contrast during discussion.

You might also choose to focus on a particular character, describing what is known about the character's personality, background, and values. The thinking is deepened by investigating how we have come to know this about the character—by what he says, how he reacts to other people, what others say about him, his facial expressions, his manner of speaking, and his tone of voice. Comparing this with the techniques used by writers to reveal the personalities of their characters encourages viewers and readers to become more conscious, informed users of the media.

We have not yet come to fully appreciate television as a powerful medium for interconnection. In time perhaps we will come to value the development of visual literacy as highly as we do textual literacy. We are not there yet.

A great deal of research is showing us that the number of hours children are spending in front of screens is increasing while the hours watching television are decreasing. Our kids do still watch television on a daily basis. Research in Australia shows that while television viewing has declined among children 0–14 years between 2001 and 2013, they are still watching on average almost two hours of free to air television per day (ACMA, 2015).

This does not include the amount of time they are viewing material on Netflix, YouTube, videos embedded in Facebook, and the like. How much do you know about this material? What are your students learning from what they are viewing? To what extent are we incorporating into their learning at school the 7.5 hours a day that our students spend being influenced by the impressions they gain from viewing screens? "Children in the United States ages 8 -18 spend on average 7.5 hours a day with media and technology screens" (AACAP, 2015).

YouTube is a rich and diverse source of video material from short amateur videos made with smart phones to polished lengthy productions. You can find eye witness videos of earthquakes as they are happening; songs, explanations, and tricks to help with multiplication; films about skyscrapers, 1066, and the Battle of Hastings; and explanations of the electoral system. In fact you can find something about almost everything on YouTube. Some of it is serious, learned, and accurate. Some of it is amusing, trivial, and just for fun. Some of it is inaccurate and some can be very offensive and disturbing. We offer many ways of keeping them safe in the digital world in a later chapter. As they get older you will want them to learn how to be discerning and how to sift through what is worthwhile and what is not.

~ Comparing a newspaper treatment of a topical story with that found on television or YouTube provides ample opportunities to think below the surface, to interrogate rather than simply assimilate. We can pose such questions as:

- Which do you find more powerful, the written word or the visual image? Why is this?

- Whose account do you trust most?
- What are some of the ways each of these media manipulate you and your own opinions?
- Where do you find the greatest amount of information?
- A day or two later, what do you recall most vividly from what you read and saw? Is this difference significant?

THE IMMIGRATES MUST ASSIMILATE

What happens if we simply accept the digital divide and leave the grown-ups largely out of the picture? It is not news to any adult that children and young people today continually challenge the status quo and the rules and regulations of the adult world. They are listening to a different generation, a different set of voices, and these voices are filled with questions because they are young, lacking experience, and hence lacking wisdom. They don't want to be told by adults. They want to work it out themselves. They no longer feel isolated from one another.

Political revolutions today are increasingly energized by the young and their ability to inform and unite with one another through social media. Demonstrations can arise almost instantaneously, as tweets become viral among a target audience and the young who are attuned to the network head to the streets to support one another and the ideas that have been promulgated and fed by the same social media.

We are slowly learning that it doesn't work to try and give young people prepackaged solutions born of our experiences. Obedience just doesn't work anymore. Rebellion and resistance to the older generation may have always been a characteristic of adolescence but it is changing now that youth has found itself as a networked entity. The "Rebel Without a Cause" is no longer an isolated teenager, but it is an interconnected generation. It is imperative that we give them the tools to find causes worthy of rebellion. What they need from us are the tools to help them navigate and to draw their own maps.

Almost every system of education in the world is now going through an attempt to realign and reform itself. We know something isn't working. The new generation has always challenged the old and the old generations have always thrown their hands up in dismay and exclaimed "What's the world coming to?" But if we don't come to a clear understanding that things are changing profoundly this time, we will fail to give our children the skills they will need to cope successfully.

The digital age is changing us. It is changing the world around us, it is changing the ways in which we do things and the ways in which we think, and the rate of change is accelerating. We need to ensure that we do lose any of our capacity to think with focus and in depth. It is also changing our plastic, versatile, adaptive, amazing brains. Our schools, and what we do within them, must reflect these changes, or become irrelevant.

KEY IDEAS IN THIS CHAPTER

- Television can be a means for interconnection just as story-telling around the fire was in preliterate times.
- While the Common Core mentions electronic media, the development of visual literacy is largely neglected.
- We can initiate classroom lessons and discussions at home that help youngsters to focus and look more closely at particular aspects of television drama thereby deepening their understanding of the medium.
- Given the amount of time young people spend with screens, it's important that they understand what they are watching at a more than superficial level.
- The digital age is giving young people a great deal more power than they had in the past.
- Adults may be struggling to keep up, but it is essential that we maintain the struggle and provide our youngsters with the tools of thought that will enable them to cope successfully.

DISCUSSION

- What goes on in your house when the television is on? Is interaction encouraged or discouraged?
- Compare the amount of time your young people spend reading and the amount of time they spend viewing. Are they being encouraged to be critical, thoughtful viewers as well as readers?
- What proportion of the curriculum is devoted to the thoughtful use of screen media?
- Which values and attitudes are young people learning from the adults around them? Are they also learning values and attitudes from electronic mass media? What about social media?
- Think of the various forms of electronic media and of social media used by the children you know. Do you see them as forces for good, as useful, and encouraging productive interaction and thoughtful behavior or something else?
- List the skills you think the adults should be teaching the youngsters if they are to become thoughtful users of digital and electronic media.

Chapter Eight

Living in Two Worlds
Tangible and Virtual

We live in many different environments, almost different worlds. Your world when you are on a camping holiday in the wilderness is vastly different from the world you inhabit when attending a high-level strategic curriculum planning meeting at school, or when having lunch with old school friends.

Most of us understand how these different worlds work and intersect. We know the appropriate clothes to wear, the language to use, the ways to sit and eat, and the level of formality in our dealings with other people. We become highly skilled at moving from one world to another even if we sometimes need a little readjustment time—returning to work after an extended holiday might be one example of this.

In this book we are considering two particular and different worlds that our young people inhabit, and they exist in both in an intricately intertwined manner and both worlds are of great importance. Both of these worlds offer profound opportunities for learning. Our task is to help maintain a productive balance between the two, and we can only do that if we really understand what is going on.

⇝ This is another big fish found in deep water—understanding how these two worlds interact.

The tangible world has been with us since we began. It includes all of the interactions with the physical world around us and the creatures within it. It is the conversations we have, the books we read, the meals we eat, the walks we take, the flowers we smell, and the chocolate we taste. It is sensory and intellectual, emotional, and tangible. For want of a better word we will call this the tangible world, conceding that it embraces much more than the things we can touch.

The second world we are considering is the digital, electronic world. Some might call it a virtual world because it mirrors so much of the tangible world but without the physical forms of the real world. It is intricate, complex, dynamic, and extraordinarily engaging.

This virtual world goes everywhere with us because we access it through our phones and tablets anywhere we have access to the Internet. Increasingly there is wifi in a growing number of public spaces, and as long as you have a phone signal, you can also access the Internet. Wherever you see young people you will see them interacting with this virtual world, usually mediated through their phones. Our involvement with our smart phones can be very intense and often it seems to decrease our awareness of the things going on around us in the tangible world. Try telling a fourteen-year-old to stop playing Minecraft or checking a Facebook feed and come down for dinner.

The virtual world is a seductive place. In many significant ways our experiences of it resemble our experiences of the tangible world. When we go out to meet our friends for coffee we are aware of the peripheral world. We watch cars pass by, we notice the breeze, we see someone we know across the road, and we are distracted by a notice in a shop window. All these things make up our experience of the real world and we make constant decisions about the extent to which we will or will not be distracted by them.

So it is in the virtual world and that is why young people feel so comfortable in this world. While we are reading the newspaper online we might follow a link to explore a side issue, we hear a ding as an email arrives, or a swish as an Instant Message pops up. When a friend posts a thought, a photo, or a piece of music on Facebook, we get a notification sound and it interests us. We are totally immersed in this ever-changing, interconnected virtual world in a way similar to our involvement in the tangible world.

THE VIRTUAL WORLD HAS ITS OWN FORM OF REALITY

Metaphors are useful and it is helpful, perhaps, to think of your device as a room. Interacting with the device is as going into the room. It is a real place. Real conversations can be had there with real people in real time—right now. But each of us goes into a different room and the rooms often do not intersect. This is apparent in the random conversations that take place when a group of young people are all "inside" their phones, but all in different places. Suddenly one exclaims, "Who knew? Scallops have 36 eyes and they are all blue." Another says "Barak Obama has just made another speech," which is responded to in turn by "Hey, check out this cat in a Santa costume." Each of these young people is in a second world and the worlds do not overlap.

This kind of socializing bears no resemblance to the kinds of "hanging out with friends" engaged in by their parents and it only becomes a problem when it *replaces* us all being in the same "world" at the same time.

We need to guard against the tangible world becoming simply a resource for the virtual world. We were recently told a story by someone who had been in St Peter's square just after the election of a new Pope on two different occasions. The first time was many years ago and the crowds had gathered to welcome this new Pope and express their appreciation. As he appeared on the balcony, there was a huge wave of cheering and applause that filled the piazza. He was also fortunate enough to be in Rome when Pope Francis was elected and again took himself to St Peter's to experience this momentous day. As the Pope appeared he was immediately aware of something totally different from his first experience.

The crowd was so quiet, and there was hardly any applause. A quick look around him revealed the cause—you can't applaud when one hand is holding up a smartphone taking a video.

The appearance of the Pope has become the raw material for the creation of a virtual world, when the videos are watched later at home. The tangible world becomes seen as the source of content for the virtual world.

We find ourselves taking selfies so we can put them on Facebook, and we attend events and watch them through our smartphone video cameras so we can record them and watch them again in our virtual world. We step out of the most intense real-life experiences in order to post an update to Facebook. As a friend recently said, "If it's a beautiful sunset and I don't post a photo of it on Facebook, is it still a beautiful sunset?"

We can teach our kids how to move between the virtual life and the tangible life. Just as we have to learn how to leave the office behind when we go on vacation, we need to help our youngsters to find balance between the superengaging virtual world and the tangible world. Small children can react with unexpected distress or even rage when forced to put away a digital device. We don't need to do much to encourage complete engagement with that world. But we do need to find ways to encourage children and young adults to fully engage with the tangible world, to put the devices away completely for a time.

We want to look for ways in which the Internet and our devices can be resources for the real world rather than vice versa. If we want people to come and join us on a walk in the forest we can use the Internet to get them there. If we want to know the names of certain plants we pass as we walk, we could use an app to add to our experience of the real world. Rather this than the tangible world simply becoming a resource for the Internet world of Stumbleupon, Pinterest, and Instagram.

BACK TO PHYSICAL REALITY

In the classroom let's begin with physical experiences whenever possible, rather than beginning with something virtual.

In the Common Core State Standards we read that in science literacy in grades 6–8 students should "Compare and contrast the information gained from experiments, simulations, video, or multimedia sources with that gained from reading a text on the same topic" (CCS, 2009. ELA-LITERACY.RST.6–8.9). It is quite deliberate that "experiments" come first in the list because direct experience is particularly powerful.

Involvement with the virtual world can make us lose contact with the tangible world in remarkable ways. Watch someone walking along the footpath looking at their phone screen and see how frequently they almost or actually bump into things. How many people have been astounded at how much time has passed while they were on the net and they feel that they haven't actually "done" anything? Kids forget to eat and sleep because they are so wrapped up in their games. People have lost their lives because of their superengagement with the virtual world and their inability to ignore a text message that comes in while they are driving. The virtual world can so easily overwhelm the tangible world.

THE VIRTUAL WORLD AS A RESOURCE

We would do well to focus on ways in which the virtual world can provide a resource for the tangible world rather than vice versa. There are applications (or apps), for example, that map the stars we look at in the night sky. The act of looking up into a night sky and seeing the Milky Way is powerful beyond description. It tells us something profound about our place in the universe. It is far more impressive than apps where we can stay indoors and see an animated, virtual version.

We can show our city children pictures of the Milky Way, and they can explore the constellations on a tablet or a computer screen. But nothing matches the experience of standing in the blackness of night and looking up. It isn't unreasonable to wonder how our understanding of our own place in the universe is influenced by whether or not we are able to witness first-hand the immensity of the universe.

We can show a child a picture of a giraffe and describe its height but that will be pale in comparison to that same child standing on the other side of the fence at the zoo and looking up to see the giraffe's head towering above. Reading about the germination of seeds and bulbs is one thing. Watching it happen in front of you is something else entirely, especially if you have had the opportunity to get earth under your nails and to smell the sweet richness of the soil as you planted the bulb.

THE CASE FOR BALANCE

Let's teach our kids how to live fully in both worlds. They need to understand that while they are immersed in their virtual world, the tangible world is going on and changing and they have to find and reinforce their place within it. They need to understand the importance of disconnecting from the virtual enough to re-enter the tangible, but also to see how the tangible and the virtual connect.

It's not a case of one world being good and the other being bad.

We need to be in control of both worlds and be able to exist affirmatively in each. When kids send intimate pictures of themselves on the Internet they are acting within a virtual world. They get into trouble when these same pictures suddenly appear in the tangible world. What seems to be acceptable in one world is n't necessarily acceptable in the other.

On dating sites people feel the power of the virtual because they can recreate themselves as virtually anyone they please. They can create a new persona and become who they wish they were rather than who they actually are. The personalities they create interact with the personalities other people create in the virtual world. Relationships are built. Problems only arise when tangible and virtual worlds meet.

The emails we receive may be part of the digital, virtual world but they have implications for what we do and come from people in the tangible world. The speed and ease with which an email can be sent easily outpaces our capacity for thoughtful reflection. Many a "send" button has been pressed and then instantly regretted. With a letter there was always a space between the writing and the posting.

The issue for our kids is not that one world is good and the other is bad, or one is real and the other is pretend. Both worlds are significant and valuable.

We were sitting recently in a doctor's waiting room. Next to us was a young boy of eight or nine completely absorbed in a shoot-em-up game on his tablet. His back was bent over and his eyes were glued to the screen in total, absorbed focus. People came and went, and the ladies behind the reception desk asked questions, offered advice, and gave people forms to fill in. The doctors came out from time to time to usher their patients into their consulting rooms. The boy saw none of this. He was totally occupied killing aliens.

How do we learn about the world and how it operates? We learn much by observing—by watching and listening to the people around us and by trying to make sense of what we see and hear. But what is this lad seeing and hearing? What world is he striving to make sense of? A world full of aliens, where his job is to shoot them.

Would we have minded so much if he had sat there absorbed in a book? Might we not have been pleased to see him engaged in such a traditional and respected activity? Perhaps, but there is a significant difference between the involvement we achieve when reading a book and when we are shooting aliens on a tablet.

When we read, we set the pace. When we play a shoot-em-up on a tablet, the game sets the pace. We know that if we lift our eyes from the page of a novel, when we look down it will still be exactly as we left it, we can re-enter its world exactly where we were before we looked up. Not so with a video game. A momentary lapse of concentration might see me dead or missing magic charms, extra powers that can popup out of nowhere, or suddenly ambushed by a whole new set of aliens. I am the player, but I am not entirely in control. The level of engagement in these games is of a very different order from the level of engagement in the most engrossing book. Just to stay in the game the player needs to remain totally disengaged from the environment and everything going on around.

THE TANGIBLE AND THE VIRTUAL— BOTH PART OF THE REAL WORLD

The pace of cultural change has picked up exponentially with the development of the Internet. Sitting in a tram recently, on its way to Melbourne University and filled with young, fresh-faced students, we were struck by the similarity of their postures. There they sat, ear buds in ears, smart phones in hand, and with thumbs hovering over virtual keyboards. As they watched their phones, with occasional glances out the tram window presumably to make sure they didn't miss their stops, these young people were enmeshed in a web of communication that had nothing to do with where they were or who was around them physically.

It is understandable to see this as a kind of disconnection from the real world. They don't make eye contact with the other people on the tram, and they hardly look out the windows.

But we would be wrong if we saw it this way. They were communicating with people in other trams or in houses, walking along streets, sipping coffee in cafes, anywhere but here in *this* tram. The messages they were receiving may have been trivial or they may have been profound. They were in constant communication and each interaction was having its own subtle influence on them. Probably none of them was communicating with a parent.

The community has escaped the bounds of the here and now. Our youngsters are engaged in the present moment with a community that could be physically anywhere on the planet, and this is a profound change.

This means that our young people are enmeshed in a communication web for much of the time, but that web is digital, electronic, and not the physical world that surrounds them here and now. The digital world is no less real than the physical world, and it is no less important or relevant to their lives.

But it is different, and we are losing a great deal if we allow it to *replace* the physical world. Chatting on social media has none of the nonverbal nuance that we know carries a significant amount of meaning in face-to-face conversations. Short textual messages shuttled back and forth allow little or no time for thought about carefully chosen words, Give no quarter when a message is misconstrued, or when feelings are inadvertently hurt. Social media has a significant and valuable place in the world, but it isn't the best choice everywhere.

Our task is to ensure that the divide between the digital world and the tangible world does not become so large that one side or the other loses its value and its importance. We do not want to find ourselves with our children on one side of the divide and the teachers and parents on the other side, neither able to comfortably jump the gap. As "LOL" and "OMG" enter the spoken repertoire we need to be alert for this injection of a kind of shorthand speech, useful in its place but lacking the clarity and precision that powerful communication demands.

THE VIRTUAL WORLD AND SURFACE THINKING

Many of these changes tend to encourage surface thinking. The constant, social digital interactions that our kids engage in mean that they are bombarded with an enormous quantity of information and influences. Impressions, momentary experiences, and the shorthand conversations on SMS and Twitter are squeezing out in-depth conversations.

As adolescents our generation would spend hours on the phone talking. Today? Young people rarely write letters, they tend not to use email, and they are much less likely to phone one another. Instead they "chat." And there lies the problem.

YOU REALLY NEED SOMETHING MORE THAN AN SMS CHAT TO THINK DEEPLY ABOUT SOMETHING

We know that the nonverbal aspects of conversation carry significant amounts of meaning. Tone of voice, physical posture, facial expressions, all of these add important information to the words spoken. All of these disappear when the communication is digital and at a distance.

Reducing a letter written to a friend, describing a recent school field trip, to a 140-character Twitter message or an SMS is a useful way of demonstrating the limitations of this form of communication. The discussion that follows, where you consider the things that had to be left out, will be the opportunity to think below the surface, to examine the medium. This could be followed up by considering the kinds of messages that are most suited to SMS or Twitter. Would you use Twitter to arrange a meeting with a friend? Is it an appropriate medium to break up with a girlfriend? Is it wise to apologize to someone by SMS?

When studying a particular region of the country we might head for the library and collect a set of books with information about the area we are considering. Using pictures, maps, charts, and the like we can impart a lot of information.

How much more powerful it would be if your group of children was also able to use Skype or Facetime to talk to children living in this part of the country, to listen to them talk, to ask them about how they live, and what they do differently. Facebook allows you to go live with video and sound. What a powerful medium this is when trying to really understand someone else and their way of life.

If you want youngsters to learn something about the variety of plant life in your area, don't begin by researching on the Internet. Begin by going to an area of uncultivated wasteland, a place filled with weeds and variety. Then take a trip to someone's garden. Having explored and perhaps described and categorized an aspect of the physical world, they can turn to the virtual world of the Internet to gain further information. Then the learning becomes deeper because we have melded the physical world with the virtual world and they both lend their richness to our understanding.

LEARNING IN THE BACK SEAT

When our children were young and we went somewhere by car, they sat in the back seat. If the trip was anything longer than a visit to the local supermarket the antics in the back seat were pretty predictable. A lot of the time they would be looking out the window, taking in the scenery. They would be watching the world going by—and learning a bit about it through the window. There may have been some conversation going on too, between the front and the back seat, or between the siblings. Inevitably, if it was a long trip an argument would eventually erupt. Someone would be taking up too much of the seat or the armrest, or someone would be making irritating noises.

The disagreement would be negotiated, with a little help from the front seat if necessary. Perhaps some guidelines would be laid down or maybe a reminder of expected behavior would be presented together with a few consequences.

There would be a lot of learning going on in that car—learning about the environment in which we lived, about how cities change as we travel through them, about the differences between our suburb and others, about how to get along, and how to settle disagreements. It was interaction on a grand scale with the physical world and all its variations and complexities. On a particularly long trip we would need to find ways to amuse ourselves, to evade boredom. We would play games or read books.

What happens today? Increasingly the back seat resembles the tram we mentioned earlier in this chapter—eyes glued to the screen of the smart phone and ears filled with music. These children of the contemporary back seat are barely in the car at all. They are enmeshed in a digital, virtual world. They are listening to each other, not to us, the adults. With their focus on the digital world they don't see what is outside the window, they don't overhear the conversations of the adults in the front seats, they fail to notice the road signs, the behavior of the other drivers, the way their own car manoeuvers on the highway, and the way the driver controls what is happening. They are missing so much.

THE WORLD IS A FASCINATING AND DANGEROUS PLACE—DON'T MISS ANYTHING

This ability to stay utterly focused is a strength in the right circumstances. Watch the number of split second decisions a child makes when playing one of these games. His brain is in rapid fire mode, weighing up the importance of a multitude of factors, learning from previous experience with the game and predicting the consequences of every subsequent move. This is powerful stuff, flexible, dynamic thinking all in the context of a game. The game may be basically trivial but the thinking skills that are being developed are anything but trivial.

We see children involved like this with tablet games in restaurants, on public transport, in cars, anywhere that adults want a bit of peace and quiet. It is so easy to keep a child occupied with a tablet. But the world is going on around them and they are not a part of it, and so they are not learning about it. The issue here is not the technology and not the game. It's the context.

What is this child missing out on if she doesn't play these games? We would suggest that she is missing out on opportunities to develop a level of mental agility that could be very useful, opportunities to think on the run, to make split second decisions. But if the context is such that by playing a game she is disengaged from opportunities for social learning then she may well be missing out on some other very important lessons, about how to function in a richly diverse and dynamic society.

Children's game playing is building up some very valuable thinking skills. But, as with most things in life, moderation is the key. These games only become a problem when they displace a children's engagement with the tangible world going on around them.

VIRTUAL AND PHYSICAL SEEING AND TOUCHING

The plasticity of the brain means that it is constantly in the process of being reformed and "rewired" according to the kinds of experiences we are having. Babies, for example, develop three-dimensional vision not simply because of the physical development of their eyes. They learn it through their interactions with the three-dimensional world as their brains learn how to integrate and interpret their sensory experiences with the world around them. The muscles of the eye are strengthened every time the baby changes his locus of focus from something close by to something distant.

There is a brand of bouncing baby chair that has a special holder for an electronic tablet so that a premobile baby can be amused by watching videos. What is a baby in this chair, looking at a screen, learning about the three-dimensional world if significant periods of time are spent watching a two-dimensional illusion that rapidly skips from one image to the next? How are the baby's eye muscles being strengthened when the locus of focus is fixed at a spot only a few inches away? How is this baby's brain being molded and wired?

Babies learn a great deal about the physical characteristics of objects by handling them. Block play is very important for babies because they learn how to manipulate things, how to control their own fingers and hands as they place blocks, and how to plan for the next step in building a tower. Anyone who has watched a small child building a tower is often impressed by the persistence demonstrated. Each time the tower collapses the child gathers the blocks up and tries again. But we know that different children can have very different capacities for persistence in this task. Some will keep on trying, making small adjustments after each failure until the tower is as high as possible. Others will soon scream in frustration and send the blocks flying across the floor.

But blocks get all over the floor and are sometimes painfully trodden on by adults. How much easier it must be to give a child a tablet with a tower-building app with which to play. By sliding his fingers across his screen he can move these illusory blocks around and build a tower. But the important thing is that it is all an *illusion* and teaches very little about the physical world, its properties, and how to effectively interact with and within it.

The parts of this baby's plastic brain that deal with spatial relationships, coordination, and hand and eye movements are developing to cope with an illusory world. Danger arises when these illusory experiences crowd out the opportunities for the baby to experience and gradually exercise control over the physical world.

TAKING A BREATHER

The frenetic pace of this interconnected world can sometimes feel overwhelming. We know that the incidence of depression and stress-related illnesses is increasing dramatically in the developed world. There is a growing interest in the concept of mindfulness as a possible antidote to the levels of stress that can seriously inhibit our ability to function optimally.

The fascination and ever-changing nature of the shallows can keep us engaged and excited for long periods of time. Time flies so quickly and you intended to only spend a few minutes checking your Facebook feed, or got caught up with the hyperlinks in the article you were reading. The brain jumps from one web page to another. It's exhausting!

We need to disengage from this world of constant distraction and spend time in deeper thought and contemplation. This doesn't come easily or naturally for many children. They need to be taught how to do this. Many schools and families are exploring the practice of mindfulness as a tool to slow down the mind and enable it to find the focus and peace it needs to deliberately pay attention to just one or two things.

The Oxford Mindfulness Centre (OMC) is an internationally recognized body within Oxford University's Department of Psychiatry. It describes its programs as opportunities for those "who are struggling to keep up with the constant demands of the modern world" and teaches people how to engage in mindful meditation and "pay attention on purpose."

The development of mindfulness requires us to disentangle from the swirling flood of information and interconnected thoughts that sometimes seem to engulf us, to focus on one thing rather than allowing the wanderings of our restless minds to dominate out thinking.

> It sounds and is simple, but it is remarkably hard to do. Especially in our modern task-focused lives we don't know how to pay wise attention to what we are doing, so we miss whole swathes of our lives, and easily get caught in over-thinking—damaging our well-being and making us depressed and exhausted. (OMC)

Similarly in the United States the University of Massachusetts Medical School (UMMS), Center for Mindfulness researches and provides education in mindfulness for both members of the public and health professionals. Once again, the focus is on teaching people how to disengage for periods of time from the hurly burly of life and the sometimes frantic activity of the mind (UMMS).

Our youngsters can become so enmeshed in the nets of the digital world that it is essential that the adults teach them how to recognize these nets for what they are. They must learn how to make positive use of the potential for interaction and integration, but also how to disentangle themselves on a regular basis so that they can pay focused attention to things and explore more deeply, without the distractions that the digital surface provides.

STAYING IN THE MOMENT—OR STOPPING TO LOOK AROUND

Consider this recent train journey. At the first stop a young woman got into the carriage and sat opposite. At first it appeared she must be listening to her radio or mp3 player but there was no evidence of ear buds. So what was it that caused the subtle, soft smiles to flit across her face from time to time? Why did her lips move, almost imperceptibly as if in a silent conversation with someone inside her head? Was she talking to someone inside her head? We have no idea. We do know that by having the opportunity to spend time in a carriage with her, where we noticed her and wondered about her, we were somehow enriching our understanding of people.

Behind us we could hear the interminable questions and comments of a very small boy. Every now and then he would erupt into cries and protests and each time his mother responded calmly, with words that we could not distinguish, only their patient tone. When they finally alighted and walked toward the exit gate and past our carriage we saw how young the mother was, and how she was still chatting to her little boy. We commented that her journey would have been so much more peaceful had she given him a digital game to play with. Just think how much he would have missed out on. Among other things he would also have missed out on the opportunity to understand something about intellectually disabled people.

Also in our carriage was a small family—a mother and her two adult sons. We quickly came to understand something about them by recognizing a number of cues—the volume at which they spoke, the sorts of questions they asked each other, the ways in which one of them obsessed over a seemingly minor disagreement and asked the same question over and over again, finally stating quite firmly and with some intensity that, "This has made me very upset" and then sitting in silence for the rest of the journey. This little boy had the opportunity to watch and listen, to learn about the varieties that make up our human family.

Listening to and attempting to participate in dinner table discussions are how children learn the art of conversation. They learn how to respect the opinions of others, how to disagree politely, how to build a discussion by adding to what someone else has said, they learn how to take turns, how to make jokes, and which jokes are appropriate. How often, when you dine out, do you see children immediately take out their electronic games as soon as they sit down?

We are not suggesting there is no place for such devices when children are in social situations. When our children were young we would often take some books or colored pencils with us when we went out visiting or to a restaurant for dinner. It's about balance.

Let's give the kids some time to learn how to be social beings too. Bringing out the tablet early on might ensure Mum and Dad may have a peaceful dinner, but they will be abdicating one of their primary responsibilities—teaching their children how to behave in society.

We cannot truly understand anything if we fail to pay it due attention. So it is with the society around us. For children to understand the world rather than simply experience it minute by minute, they need to be keen observers. As they develop the capacity to observe they will also begin to understand the world in greater depth.

KEY IDEAS IN THIS CHAPTER

- Today we can live in two worlds—the physical and the virtual. It is the adults' task to help children achieve balance as well as learn how to live fully in both.
- Both worlds have their own kind of reality.

- It is easy for the virtual world to lead to surface thinking because it is so immersive and so fast.
- The virtual world is very compelling and so we need to be careful we don't let it supplant the physical world.
- As they learn how to move between the physical and the virtual, youngsters also need to learn that the virtual world is a resource for the real world and not vice versa.
- The speed of the virtual world tends to encourage surface thinking.
- Mindfulness recognizes the need to slow down and to focus.

DISCUSSION

- How much do the young people you know live their lives online?
- Are their online lives different in any significant way from their physical lives? If you asked them, would they look at things differently from you? If you have the opportunity—ask them.
- When you do research online, formally or informally, how do you interact with the Internet? Do you forge ahead, staying with the one source you find? Do you compare several sources, and if so, how? What do you do with the hyperlinks?
- Can you recall researching something in a library? Was your interaction with the information the same as when you carry out digital research?
- When a child asks you a question, where do you look first for an answer? Do you look to your own experience, a book, Wikipedia, or Google?
- Do you recall long trips in the car with children? What was going on in the back seat? What might have been missed?

Chapter Nine

The Best of Both Worlds

The digital world sometimes tempts us into becoming binary thinkers rather than deep thinkers. Deciding between two things is relatively simple. The problem is that most important things in life are far more complex than that. An effective thinker understands this and is able to consider more than two options. Let's look at one example.

Keyboards are everywhere. We marvel at the speed with which kids manage to pump out text on a full-sized keyboard or with their thumbs on a smart phone. In the United States there is a growing debate about whether or not children need to be formally taught cursive writing. The Common Core State Standards (CCSS) do not mandate its teaching. Although the CCSS for writing state that from kindergarten children should be "drawing, dictating and writing," the kindergarten standards only mention the need to:

> explore a variety of digital tools to produce and publish writing, including in collaboration with peers. (CCSS.ELA-LITERACY.W.K.6)

And in grade 4,

> demonstrate sufficient command of keyboarding skills to type a minimum of one page in a single sitting. (CCSS.ELA-LITERACY.W.4.6)

The amount able to be typed is expected to increase year by year. Nowhere is there any mention of the need to explicitly teach handwriting. There has been much debate about the removal of the requirement to teach a fast, fluent, legible form of handwriting in schools. Some states have decided to reintroduce this—Tennessee is one such state where cursive writing has been reintroduced at grade 2.

In Australia we have seen frequent discussions about the problems faced by final-year high-school students being required to write extended passages long hand in exams, when they are unused to the practice during their school year. They feel they lack fluency and their hands ache! A recent examination by us of some hand-written questionnaires completed by year 12 students in Australia demonstrated a significant lack of fluency and legibility.

Have you ever been troubled by the weird and wonderful ways in which young adults hold pens and pencils? They look awkward and these youngsters will revert to keyboards as soon as practicable. It used to be that when we taught grade 1 and 2 children, part of the curriculum was directed toward teaching them how to hold their pencils efficiently and how to form letters that would lead to fluent, legible, effortless handwriting.

There are those who regard this particular learning process as a waste of time, as an example of people clinging to an old, outmoded technology. How often do we set things that are essentially different up against each other for comparison and competition?

- Which is better, the movie or the book?
- Which side of the brain is most important, the left or the right?
- Who are smarter, men or women?
- Which do you prefer, oysters or chocolate cake?
- Which is better, a photographic or a painted portrait?

THIS BINARY THINKING OFTEN DOESN'T WORK

Neither does the question, "Which should we teach, keyboarding (virtual handwriting) or handwriting (physical handwriting)?" This is not a competition between the old print-dominated technologies and the technologies of the new digital age. There will always be a place for the handwritten, just as there will always be a place for the painted.

Just because a child can easily take a photograph of a tree doesn't mean that we should not give him the opportunity to draw or paint a tree. There is something about the artist that is revealed in a painting, a personal response to the subject matter, and a reinterpretation of the literal truth that comes about when a subject is painted or drawn. So it is with handwriting.

We know that every person's handwriting is unique. The keyboard gives us the vocabulary and the syntax. The pen gives us something of the person. Another manifestation of the marvelous variations between people can be seen in the formal, controlled, and perfectly formed handwriting of one person, the tight, tiny, cramped writing of another, and the expansive, impetuous scrawl of yet another. Our handwriting is one of the things that proclaims our individuality.

How many of us hold dear the early attempts of our children to write us notes, the love letters of an early sweetheart, or even the handwritten name of a long dead loved one in a favorite book of poems?

We sometimes seem to be very good at throwing out our babies with the bath water in education. Let's not do it again. Let's not view this as a competition at all. Just as the 140 characters of a twitter post has its own value, just as email is a powerful contributor to communication and how we get things done in a fast-paced world, just as Google gets us information in a matter of seconds, so is handwriting an important part of expressing who we are. Let's continue to teach our children the intimate, expressive art of handwriting as well as the efficient, expedient skill of keyboarding.

Two researchers at Indiana University reported that when preliterate children write letters by hand three areas of the brain are activated, the same ones that are activated in adulthood when we read and write—the reading neural circuits. This was demonstrated by carrying out functional magnetic resonance imaging scans. Children who typed or traced letters, however, didn't activate these areas (James and Engelhardt, 2013, pp 32–42).

It has also been demonstrated that children who handwrite have greater neural activation in the working memory and that handwriting tends to produce more words and original ideas than those produced using a keyboard (Berninger, 2012).

When we learn to write fluently we are integrating sensation, movement control, and thinking. The gradual movement from messiness and lack of control of the writing implement to clarity and fluency in handwriting reflect neural changes taking place during the learning process.

Learning how to write changes our brains in ways that using a keyboard does not and it would appear that these changes are beneficial for learning in general.

Interesting research has examined the differences in learning outcomes resulting from note taking that is long hand and note taking on laptops. Students from two campuses of the University of California, Los Angeles, and from Princeton University were given a series of tests examining the differences in their learning when they took notes from fifteen-minute TED videos. Some students wrote their notes long hand and others used laptops. The results are sobering.

Students taking notes on their laptops tended to take longer notes and these notes were more frequently verbatim transcriptions of the words in the video material they were watching. Long-hand note takers, on the other hand, took down fewer words, were less likely to transcribe verbatim, and performed significantly better than the laptop note takers on conceptually based test questions. Even when the laptop note takers were instructed NOT to write down verbatim what they heard in the video and instead to recode it in their own words, they still tended to transcribe verbatim and the intervention made little or no difference to their poorer learning outcomes.

Why was this so? Why is it that a method that enables the recording of more content also tends to inhibit learning of conceptual material? Even when given the opportunity to review their notes later and before being tested, the laptop note takers performed poorly compared with their long-hand note-taking peers.

Because we cannot write as quickly as we can type, it is impossible to keep up with the speed of speech in the lecture situation. Taking long-hand notes requires us to engage in significantly more mental processing as we evaluate and summarize what we are hearing in order to select the most important details to write in our notes. It is this mental effort that engages thinking at a deeper level and enhances our learning (Mueller and Oppenheimer, 2014).

Research at the University of Waterloo in Canada strongly suggests that typing with both hands makes writing too fast and too easy and interferes with the quality of the end product (Medimorec and Risko, 2016). Subjects were required to produce written passages firstly by typing with both hands and then typing with only one hand. Textual analysis revealed that passages typed with both hands tended to display simpler vocabulary, less complex sentences, and a poorer sense of cohesion. When subjects were required to type with only one hand—to slow down—they found a positive effect on the range of vocabulary, the complexity of the ideas, and the overall cohesion of the writing. It would seem that by slowing the process of writing down we are able to incorporate the thinking processes at a higher level.

By Slowing Down We Can Think More Deeply

It's not a case of either-or.

A major part of the problem we face in adapting to these new digital technologies arises from the tendency to think of them as replacements for things we have done differently up until now. This kind of thinking is superficial.

Texting is not the same as talking to a friend, Wikipedia isn't the same as the Encyclopaedia Britannica, cutting and pasting from Google isn't the same as writing an essay, flicking from hyperlink to hyperlink isn't the same as researching a subject, keyboarding isn't the same as handwriting and a handwritten letter isn't the same as an email, and skimming a page on a computer screen for information isn't the same as reading a book from cover to cover.

Taking notes with a laptop may not be the same as taking notes long hand, but that does not mean we should ban the laptop from the classroom. Instead we need to understand what the laptop can and cannot do well. The fast typist is able to record a vast amount of information for later review, but without the later review it is likely that the act of recording in itself may have limited the amount of learning that would have been possible had the notes been taken long hand.

The power of digital technology lies entirely in *how* we use it. If the typed notes are taken away and then summarized and rewritten in our own words, then we are engaging in that deeper level of cognitive engagement that makes learning and significant thinking about the material possible.

KEY IDEAS IN THIS CHAPTER

- Binary thinking is surface thinking.
- Curriculum developers have succumbed to the simplicity of binary thinking by comparing keyboarding and virtual writing with handwriting and deciding one is better than the other.
- In many places handwriting is no longer taught. The focus is on keyboarding.
- Handwriting is expressive of the individual.
- Different areas of the brain are activated when we handwrite and when we keyboard.
- Handwriting integrates sensation, movement control, and thinking in a more complex way than does keyboarding.
- Keyboarding is fast and students tend to take longer, more verbatim notes.
- Handwriting is slower and so we need to evaluate and summarize more when taking notes.
- Keyboarding is a fast, efficient way of recording information. Rewriting and summarizing what has been captured is what leads to deeper thinking.
- We need them both.

DISCUSSION

- Do you think it is a part of the school's responsibility to help parents work with their children on Internet use?
- Have you encountered any specific problems for the children you teach that arose out of their use of the Internet?
- Can your students write fluently and legibly with a pen or pencil? If the answer is "yes," how did they learn? How explicit was their teaching? If the answer is "no," does it matter?
- Consider some of the ways in which you can use the virtual world to broaden or deepen a student's understanding of some aspect of the tangible world.

- What differences do you see between reading a very involving book, watching a engaging movie, and playing an exciting video game? What are the strengths of each activity?
- How much time do your students spend interacting in the virtual world—researching things on the Internet, reading and responding on social media, texting and instagraming? How do they spend their free time?

Chapter Ten

Safe Enough to Think

Keeping Children Safe and Ensuring Safety of Information

Look again at the photograph of the child in the front of the book. She is all set to explore the shallows. She has her mask so she can see the wonders there, her snorkel so she can stay in the midst of the shallow water action without having to surface for breath, and a pair of flippers to help her move agilely among the bright fish.

What does she need if she is to venture safely into the deeper waters? Is the child in the photograph ready? No, she is not. Most importantly, she should not go into these deeper waters alone. This child needs an adult who is competent and capable, and has the skills not only to swim in the deep water, but to take care of a novice swimmer.

Some ground rules will be carefully communicated before anyone enters the water. The adult will make sure the child both understands and agrees with these rules. In particular they will want to both understand what to do if the child should feel unsure or unsafe at any time.

If we want our children to be effective, deep thinkers in this digital world we must ensure that they feel safe and are safe in the environments they inhabit. Creative, flexible thinking assumes the preparedness to take risks with ideas, to challenge and push some intellectual boundaries. We can only do this when we feel secure and until we feel confident enough in our own abilities, we need the guidance and sometimes the presence of an adult who knows what's going on.

There are thinking skills to be learned in order to be a deep water thinker, but when this deeper thinking is being carried out in the digital environment it is essential we make sure our children are safe.

We want to ensure that the material they encounter is safe. We don't want them exposed to pornography, excessive violence, or anything else that is inappropriate for their age and stage of development. But we also don't want them exposed to information that is deceptive, inaccurate, or manipulative until they are able to discern for themselves the qualities of the materials they encounter on the Internet.

IT'S OUT OF CONTROL AND IT'S SCARY!

Many of our young people have little or no knowledge of the privacy settings possible on their social media accounts. Many of their parents don't even know there are privacy settings! We talk to our children about stranger danger, about inappropriate touching, about the places where it is safe to be, and the places to avoid in the city. We explain the importance of having a buddy when going to a party, about the dangers of alcohol and drugs, and about the ways to behave if your date has been drinking and now wants to drive you home. In the physical world we are pretty good at teaching our children how to be safe and how to behave. Who is teaching them about chat rooms, about texting photographs of themselves to their friends, about the dangers of identifying their address or giving a phone number on a social network site?

We visited a primary school recently and the children had tablets and smartphones on their tables connected to the Internet. The teacher expected her students to make use of the resources available, "Don't forget to use your online dictionary if you are not sure of a word, and remember the web sites we bookmarked in case you want to check up on some of the information."

These were children in grade 2. Many of them had brought their own devices from home and others were using those provided by the school. The goal in this school is to embed the technology in the children's learning to such an extent that these devices are no more remarkable than a book or a piece of paper and a pencil.

The Common Core State Standards are clear. The introduction to the Language Arts Standards states that in order to be college and career ready:

> Students employ technology thoughtfully to enhance their reading, writing, speaking, listening, and language use. They tailor their searches online to acquire useful information efficiently, and they integrate what they learn using technology with what they learn offline. They are familiar with the strengths and limitations of various technological tools and mediums and can select and use those best suited to their communication goals.

We expect that our young people will learn in school those things that will equip them to be successful when they leave school—to make them college and career ready of course, but also to make them *life ready*. We are concerned with the skill that underlies every kind of learning—from science and mathematics to art and music—the ability to think and to understand.

A few nights later we attended a public forum at a local high school. The subject was cyber safety. You could almost taste the anxiety. A big subject was sexting—kids taking photos of their "girl and boy bits" and sending them to each other. Some youngsters, particularly girls, had suffered excruciating embarrassment and humiliation from this practice. Some parents felt this proved how dangerous the technology is.

But kids have written obscene notes to one another and circulated them for generations. We haven't blamed the paper and pencil. Rumors have been whispered and spread about sexual behavior and many an innocent young person's reputation has been damaged thanks to the malice of a few bullies. We don't ban whispering.

The problem is not with the technology itself, nor is it that the moral and behavioral standards of our children have dropped—although they may well have changed. Lack of understanding about the technology, about its pervasive reach, and about how to take control of it are the roots of the problem.

DON'T JUST DO SOMETHING, STAND THERE

Kids say things online that they would never dream of saying in a physical encounter. A girl sends a partially naked photo of herself to her boyfriend. Once it hits the screen of the boy's phone it becomes separated from the girl who sent it. It becomes a picture, not a person, and so the immature and unthinking boy shows it to his best mate who sends it to a couple of his friends. The viral spread begins of a picture that is in one sense becoming more and more anonymous and removed from the girl whose image it is, but at the same time has her name tagged to it.

If the girl had handed her boyfriend a similar physical photo, one of two things would be likely to happen. He would respect the girl's trust in him and her right to privacy and keep the photo safe and out of public view. If he were less discreet, he might show it to a friend or two. The important thing is that the photo would probably remain in his possession and there would never be hundreds of copies circulating among strangers as there can be with sexting.

We owe it to our children to teach them how to stay in control. Staying in control can only happen when we really know what we are doing—and that takes thought.

THE PROBLEM ISN'T THE TECHNOLOGY

We will not bridge this digital generational divide and make sure our youngsters are safe enough to think until we overcome this negative view of technology. Rarely in the history of civilization is new technology the problem. The problems arise from how we use it.

It is no different with digital technologies. A brick can be used to build the walls of a hospital, it can be thrown through a jeweler's shop window or it can be used to knock a person senseless. It's all about how we use it.

In the same way, if we do not make the effort to understand these digital technologies, from email, to Facebook, to twitter and Stumble Upon and whatever comes next, we will never learn how to direct their use in positive directions.

For the average child in primary school in the developed world there have always been smartphones, people have always texted and there have always been touch screens they can manipulate. This is not new technology to them. It is simply how the world is.

These technologies have roared out of the woods and taken over so much of our lives so quickly that we haven't learned how to deal with them. Our lack of good manners and decent behavior in dealing with them isn't the fault of the technology. We just haven't had the time yet to develop a digital etiquette, a set of acceptable behaviors. Sexting isn't the fault of the smartphone, Twitter, Facebook, or the digital camera. It's the kids who are sexting and it's them with whom we need to talk, because the problem is their behavior. Until someone explains to them clearly what the dangers are, they will continue to get themselves into trouble. It's bullying we need to address, not just sexting.

NEW WAYS TO REBEL

Rebellion is a beast of many colors. Thoughtless rebellion rarely produces anything other than trouble. Thoughtful rebellions can change the world into a better place.

If our young people are learning more of their values from one another than they did in the past, they also have a new platform for rebellion. Meeting on the corner to hang out and feed one another's dissatisfactions with the values of the past is old hat now.

Generations of parents have tried hard to control their children's circles of friends, limiting them to those they deemed most suitable. Not wanting their children to mix with "the wrong sort" was all about trying to ensure their children absorbed and carried on the values of their parents.

Today our young people are mixing with anyone they want, without parental guidance or censorship. They do it in the privacy of their rooms, on the bus or train, at the shopping mall—anywhere they have their phones. And they have their phones everywhere.

In the past, rebellion against the values of a home where the parents dominated was a dangerous business because it was often a pretty solitary business. A fourteen-year-old girl wants to go to a party and her parents say "no." In the pre-smartphone era she would have stormed off to her bedroom, perhaps put on some loud music, and seethed alone. Not today. Today she will probably still storm up to her bedroom, but then she will be online, complaining and plotting with her friends. Her anger and sense of injustice will be validated and deepened as she and her other fourteen-year-old, inexperienced and often unwise young friends elaborate and reinforce their own independent notions of what is right and wrong, what is fair and what is not.

We saw the ability of digital technology to spread rebellion during the Arab Spring. It works just the same way in the teenage bedroom.

The power to reduce the isolation of the child can also be a force for good. In the past the child who witnessed spousal abuse in the home might also seek refuge in the bedroom, perhaps shedding some tears into the pillow. The next morning, the events of the previous evening are set aside after a restorative night's sleep and the sense of distance that passing hours can bring. It's a new day, a fresh start. Similarly the youngster who was beaten by a parent often had to deal with it in isolation. A thrashing would end with banishment to the bedroom. Today there is the possibility that these traumas can be shared, and through the counsel of good friends, perhaps a way out of the misery can be found.

But what of the child who is one of the very small minority in his social group whose parents have said, "No, you can't have a phone. You are too young and we can't afford it."? For the one child in the group who cannot get online, this is tantamount to being placed "in Coventry" where no one will speak to you. These children become outsiders, excluded from the chatter, the alliances, the spats, the trends, the gossip, the jokes, and the planning of their peers. In an interconnected world it can be very tough not to have a way of connecting.

We can minimize the dangers if we encourage our young people to pull themselves away from their involvement with digital media for long enough to think carefully about what they are doing. Banning a digital device solves no problems in the long term. Discussing and thinking about the implications of a particular aspect of usage can have long-term gains.

DIGITAL MANNERS

We lack an accepted set of behavioral expectations or good digital manners. We learn how to behave by watching our parents and by being told by them how we should behave. We know, because we have been told, that it's fine to read a book on a train if you are travelling alone, but if you are travelling with a friend who wants to engage in a bit of conversation then the book needs to be put away. Our parents would call out at dinner time, "Say goodbye to your friend and come to the table" if we were chatting to a buddy on the phone.

Kids have their phones with them constantly. What is the right thing to do if the phone rings while the family is having dinner? In the past the phone was in a different room, today it is in your pocket. Nowhere is it more obvious than when you watch young people sitting around the table in a restaurant. They all have a phone and frequently one or more is using it to interact with people who are not sitting at the table. Sometimes you will see everyone at the table interacting with a phone, each in a world separate from fellow diners at their table and far, far away from the other patrons of the restaurant at the surrounding tables.

Expectations should be clear in the classroom too. When teaching university students recently, we noticed that from time to time a student would disengage from what was going on in the class to respond to something happening on her phone. Many schools have addressed this problem by simply banning phones from the school or from the classroom. Certainly it is wise to ban phones during tests. But a ban like this also removes a powerful learning tool.

It's easy to be critical. We have probably all made comments to the youngsters in our care about their use of smartphones and the death of conversation. But have you ever seriously addressed the issue with them? Have you encouraged them to *stop and think* about what they are doing?

Texting has taken over from voice calls among many teenagers. The Pew Research Center's Internet & American Life Project (2011) discovered that girls text a median of 100 texts per day. Only 35 percent of those surveyed said they actually socialized face to face with their peers outside of school. Texting is where they conduct much of their social lives. We hear of relationships being ended with a text message. Sometimes it is emotionally easier to text. If I don't see your hurt expression then I don't have to feel so bad about what I am doing, or feel responsible. But this is dangerous.

Have we taught our children how to behave in this new world? We teach our children not to bully, not to make unkind remarks about another person's appearance or way of life. But that's about talking to people, face to face. Parents tell their children that it is cruel to bully, and children see the truth of this in the face of the child they have just called "fat" or "stupid." The subtle but powerful nonverbal communication that goes on between people reinforces the truth of what their parents said.

Texting is different. A moment of anger, a thoughtless text, and the recipient might be devastated. But the sender sees none of the repercussions of that text. Who is teaching these children the rules of civil texting? What sensitivity to the feelings and rights of others might they be losing by switching from face-to-face conversations to texting?

≈ Almost all schools now have some form of antibullying program, and they address exclusion as a form of bullying. Have your students ever considered smartphone use as a potential for bullying? Pose the questions with your youngsters, and explore their answers more deeply.

Remember the grade 2 we described earlier? These children had their phones or their tablets in the classroom, they were connected to the Internet, and *they were always in full view of the teacher.* There were clearly negotiated rules in this classroom. The children knew their devices were in the room for a particular purpose and the teacher was able to monitor appropriate usage simply by being observant, because one of the non-negotiable rules was that the device was always on the table, in full view.

There are important discussions that we need to have, and we need to talk with the young people in our schools. We all do things without thinking too much of their implications. Many young people have simply not thought much about what their constant use of the phone is doing to their appreciation of the immediate, actual, physical world and their conversations with others.

THE POWER OF CONVERSATION

So much in a discussion is communicated by nonverbal cues. With social media there is nothing but the verbal and perhaps a few emojis sprinkled in. The rise and increase in number of these little images is an attempt to communicate something of the nonverbal, because we sense that we are missing something.

The ability to engage in productive, civil conversation requires a lot of face-to-face practice. We know that what we see is in many ways even more important than the words we hear. To be sensitive to these nonverbal messages both parties need to be fully present. This simply cannot be achieved through the exchange of text messages.

The value of text messaging is beyond dispute but we need to make sure we do not allow one medium of communication to dominate others to the extent of almost eliminating them. Our youngsters need to learn how to engage in constructive conversations because it is through this social process that we come to understand the communities within which we live.

The main pathway we have to understanding the complex thoughts and feelings of one another is by listening to one another. Part of education in a digital age involves coming to understand how other people think and feel. We can only achieve this if we learn how to listen and engage at length and in depth through conversation. Twitter and the SMS may be very useful media for learning succinctness, but they do little on their own to develop depth in thinking.

In the *English Language Arts Standards » Speaking & Listening* of the Common Core State Standards, from kindergarten to year 12 we read that students need to do the following:

> In kindergarten—*Follow agreed-upon rules for discussions (e.g., listening to others and taking turns speaking about the topics and texts under discussion)*

> In grade 6—*Follow rules for collegial discussions, set specific goals and deadlines, and define individual roles as needed* (CCS, 2009, ELA-LITERACY. SL.6.1.B)

> In grade 12—*Work with peers to promote civil, democratic discussions and decision-making, set clear goals and deadlines, and establish individual roles as needed* (CCS, 2009, ELA-LITERACY.SL.11–12.1.B)

You can encourage your students to think about the limitations inherent in relying too much on text-based communication by exploring the richness of nonverbal cues.

The simple act of putting emphasis on different words in a sentence can change meaning significantly. Try this: "I hate chocolate cake" or "I HATE chocolate cake" or "I hate CHOCOLATE cake" or "I hate chocolate CAKE." Each has a different meaning.

An activity where students are asked to mime different feeling states gives some powerful insights into what is NOT there when they attempt to communicate their feelings in text alone. Body stance, facial expression, volume of voice, tone of voice, gestures, speed of delivery, hesitations and pauses—all these are missing in textual online conversations.

Open up the discussion, and let the youngsters themselves explore the problems associated with constant smartphone use and come up with their own solutions. Any solution that grows from their thinking and their experiences has a greater chance of success than one simply imposed by the grown-ups.

THE DIGITAL DATING GAME

Instant networking has led to the development of a whole new set of strategies for meeting people of the opposite sex. Secondary school students are increasingly making use of sites such as Tinder and Hinge. It doesn't take them long to discover that there is no way of checking whether their given age is correct. There is also no way of checking if the descriptions of others on the site are accurate either. Youthful experimentation can quickly become dangerous. Initially they may just be curious and go no further than making online connections, but skilled predators know how to push the safety boundaries and entice an initially cautious youngster into more perilous territory.

Just as we expect our youngsters to stop and think about how they are going to get safely home from a concert, a party, a shopping trip, or a hike in unknown terrain, we should expect them to stop and think about how they will safely navigate the terrain of social networks.

Social networking is fast and therein lie its dangers. Before she knows what is happening a girl can be catapulted into a social situation, either online or in reality, if she doesn't take some time to disentangle and think more deeply about what she is doing.

A teenage girl is hanging out after school with her friends but doesn't find any of the boys to be of particular interest. She is getting a little bored with the conversation and looking for a bit of fun. She gets a call from her friend who is at the mall in a different part of town talking to one or two attractive young men. The friend suggests she leave where she is and come and join up with her. What should she do? Will it be seen as rude to leave her current friends for greener fields or will they understand?

Her mother was never faced with this dilemma so she has had no guidance there. Instead, she works it out for herself, balancing what she would like to do using her own sense of fair play, and knowledge of what her friends have done in the past in similar situations. She says her goodbyes, calls her friend, and heads off. As she walks toward the tram her phone rings and it is the boy she met last Friday evening at a football game. She had enjoyed talking with him then, they had exchanged phone numbers, and that was all. He is suggesting a different venue where there is some very good music playing.

She is making this up as she goes along. There is no generally accepted code of behavior yet that has had time to be mediated through experience and time, and yet she constantly has to make choices. The grown-ups in her life have a responsibility to help, to come to understand the dilemma she is facing time and time again, and to give her an opportunity to stop and think about what she is doing and about what she will do next time.

Teachers and parents cannot stand on the outside looking in and wringing their hands bewailing the modern age. We need to find out what is going on and then help our children to control the ways in which they interact within the digital milieu.

Even more fraught with problems are the "hook up" sites on the Internet that we have already mentioned. Some of these are reputable dating sites where people create profiles and for a fee are matched with people deemed to meet their expectations. There are also sites where the simple act of turning on the GPS facility in a smartphone will make the owner of the phone visible to others in the vicinity who are looking for company of one sort or another.

Youngsters will experiment. They always have. Only if the adults understand the ways these sites work will they be able to be the "grown-ups" in the room and provide guidance and rules for safety.

THE DIGITAL THINKER

Norman Doidge in *The Brain That Changes Itself* has written extensively about the plasticity of the brain as it "rewires" itself with every new experience (Doidge, 2007). We know, for example, that the hours of practice required to become a skilled musician actually results in the growth in physical size of the area of the brain involved in this kind of learning. In a similar way, London cab drivers, renowned for having to pass "the knowledge"—a detailed internal map of all the streets, lanes, and places in London—have a larger hippocampus than others. The hippocampus is the area of the brain involved with spatial navigation as well as the integration of short-term memory into long-term memory.

Marc Prensky suggests that extended experiences with digital media are creating a generation of young people who do not think in the linear manner of their parents to the same extent. They leap from thought to thought, reflective of the jumping from text to hyperlink and hyperlink to hyperlink on a computer or tablet screen (Prensky, 2012). Looked at optimistically, perhaps our children have become more adept at parallel processing than their predominantly linear parents' generation. A more pessimistic view might be that we are in danger of creating a generation of surface thinkers, "gist" thinkers who are either reluctant or simply do not recognize the need to think deeply.

Much has also been written about the apparent short attention spans resulting from too much television watching. This old chestnut fails when watching a child playing a computer game. The attention is focused and extended, sometimes for worryingly long periods of time. We need to consider that perhaps the issue is not simply about the ability to pay attention so much as the ability to pay particular kinds of attention. Our children's brains are changing and they seem to pay best attention when they have the opportunity to interact.

Many young parents are also a part of this switched-on, interconnected world. They are at ease with their smartphones and tablets, look forward to getting involved with virtual reality, and share their devices happily with their babies and their toddlers. We laugh at the examples of one-year-olds frustrated by glossy magazines because nothing happens when they swipe the colorful photographs.

Our children learn to talk because their brains are primed for language learning. All they need is an environment rich in talk and conversation and the opportunity to interact with it. It is gratifying to see an adult in conversation with a baby while they negotiate the aisles of the supermarket. A home rich in conversation that includes the children will provide the firmest foundation for later successful learning and the development of skilled thinking in our children, because both of these rest on language fluency.

A recent study in the United Kingdom suggests a growing problem arising from the use of electronic gadgets as a kind of babysitting service, keeping babies and children silent and still for extended periods of time. The report suggests that the ways in which these devices are being used may account to a significant extent for a 70 percent increase from 2005 to 2011 in the number of children reported to have speech and language difficulties. Instead of sitting together and talking during meal times, the family is focused on the television screen. Preschoolers are interacting with games or educational programs on their tablets rather than messily, and often inconveniently, helping a parent to prepare an evening meal. Mum or dad pushes a stroller along the street listening to music through headphones or ear buds, completely unaware of the child's exclamations, questions, or cries.

If we want our children to become skilled language users, we must talk with them a lot—whenever we can.

KEY IDEAS IN THIS CHAPTER

- Exploring in deep waters requires us to feel safe. The effective thinker feels safe enough to take risks.
- The Internet is rich in information but it is also filled with undesirable and inaccurate content. We must give our youngsters the tools to analyze and discriminate and keep them away from the undesirable.
- The technology itself is not inherently dangerous. The danger comes from how we use it.
- Young people should know how to preserve their privacy online and how to stay in control.
- Digital photos are very different from physical photos.
- Digital devices can spawn rebellion in both small and large contexts.
- We need to develop a kind of digital etiquette, a set of rules that suites each family or school.

- Secondary school students need to stop and think about the dangers inherent in various forms of social media and about the possibility of bullying and dangerous online dating.
- Thinking and language go hand in hand. The use of digital devices that restrict the use of spoken language is detrimental to the child's language development and subsequent ability to think deeply.

DISCUSSION

- If you use digital technology in your classroom what rules have you made? Do these rules solve the problems you are facing?
- How wide ranging should the use of digital media be in the classroom? Is there a use for web searches or is the library good enough? Is there a use for social media sites such as Facebook in the classroom? How might you use email or short message services in the classroom?
- How much do you know about the privacy settings on a social media site?
- College ready, career ready, life ready—where and to what extent do these three overlap?
- We accept that it is the school's responsibility to prevent bullying. How would you know if a child was being cyberbullied?
- How does the notion of "good manners" evolve? Are there any particular examples of poor digital manners that you have observed among your students?
- What have you noticed about the attention span of the young people or children with whom you interact?

Chapter Eleven

It's Hard to Manage What You Don't Understand

Some younger educators and parents may already be very familiar users of digital technology and may, in fact, be some of Prensky's "digital natives"—having grown up within the milieu of the digital age. Others may still be "digital immigrants," learning their away around and picking up the culture. Your youngsters will almost all be digital natives. School curricula incorporate that digital culture but often don't demonstrate full understanding of the magnitude of change that is happening.

EXPLORING AND PLAYING—THE BEST WAYS TO LEARN

When we introduce children to new materials and new concepts, we know how powerful it is to give them time to simply play with the stuff first. Play activates our innate curiosity and gives us the opportunity to explore without external expectations. When we are playing with something we are not concerned with failing or succeeding. We just want to play, and that is when discoveries are made.

Failure isn't an option unless we begin to compete. If we compete, it can be with ourselves or with others, but initially solitary play is all about discovery. The only requirement is that we continue to find enjoyment by discovering new things about the thing we are exploring. We discover the properties of the new object of our play and then we learn how to manipulate them in interesting and eventually more challenging ways.

Watch a child with a ball and a brick wall. Without any adult intervention or the setting of performance goals, the child will learn about the properties of the ball when it is bounced in different ways as well as the properties of her own body as she seeks to catch, hit, rebound the ball, and gradually build her mastery and repertoire of skills with the ball. As she becomes more aware of these properties she will challenge herself to perform more and more difficult and complex tasks and routines.

Adults can learn through play too. Our suggestion is, however, that you initially play with the digital device away from the temptations of competition. A youngster who has mastered the operation of a smartphone will be only too happy to demonstrate that prowess and you can very easily find yourself sucked into a competition you had never sought.

Sugata Mitra in his experiments with children in India discovered the power of play in a digital world. He explains in his book *Beyond the Hole in the Wall*, how poverty-stricken children left to their own devices with a computer will play and learn. In 1999, a computer with online access was inserted in a highly visible wall in New Delhi. Within a few hours children were surfing the web. The results were so encouraging that thirty computers were funded in this poor area of Delhi and other "computers in the wall" were installed across India.

In the years that followed Mitra's initial work, amazing results have been achieved—ten to fourteen-year-old Tamil-speaking children have taught themselves biotechnology in English and online self-organized learning environments have been set up that make the most of the ability of children to learn through play.

Some of us grew up in the age of "operation manuals." When we bought a new washing machine, chain saw, or CD player, there was a slim book that came with it explaining its operation and giving hints about how to get started. Digital devices today tend less and less to come with instructions. If you want to search online you can generally find one somewhere on the manufacturer's web site, but they are largely deemed to be unnecessary. You might find a fold-out paper "quick start" guide that helps with straightforward things such as putting in the battery or charging the device, but little more. The manufacturers expect that we will have a vague understanding of how the device works and that we will learn the rest by playing and experimenting.

Two-year-olds are notorious for resetting their parents' smartphone settings and they can barely talk, let alone read an instruction manual. If you have the opportunity, watch a baby with a tablet. You will witness purposeful play that might amaze you as the baby tries one thing after another, watching to see what the consequences are of each action and then repeating what seems to succeed, pushing each new bit of information a little further.

The more *you* play with the device, the more you will come to understand how it works and the less foreign it will feel in your hands.

ABOUT THE APPS

If you are already familiar with the operation of the device, explore the programs and apps. Play. Begin with some simple games. Solitaire and various word games proliferate as apps and many of them are completely free. Go to the app store on your device and download a game. Try it, play with it. If you don't like it you can simply delete it. These games don't take up cupboard space.

You can also open your own Facebook, Twitter, or Tumblr account and find out what it is and how it works. The Internet is a moving target. Existing networking platforms are constantly changing in subtle, and sometimes major, ways. Already we read that younger people are beginning to abandon Facebook because too many of their parents are utilizing it and it is no longer quite as "cool" as it used to be.

Nevertheless, in the United Kingdom, 91 percent of all eighteen to twenty-four-year-olds and 82 percent of all twenty-five to thirty-four-year olds hold a Facebook account and worldwide there are well over one billion people interacting on this particular platform. Our kids may move across to other apps such as WhatsApp, Viber, Instagram, or Snapchat—the list will change and grow—but we can be certain that having tasted the pleasures of social media, they will not put it down.

Choose one of these social interaction sites and start to play. Don't submit any personal details. The Internet is filled with two-dimensional characters and you can join their ranks. Facebook is like a city and you can explore it in a similar fashion. Wander about, poke into alleys and corners, open doors, and look around. It is a city filled with sign posts and doors—doors behind doors behind doors.

In these social network sites you need to keep in mind that they are just that—networks. Things are connected to one another. It's big and it's complicated, but like many big things you can easily begin in just one corner. Exploring a city can be daunting if you feel you have to explore it all, but that isn't what we do. We explore it bit by bit, neighborhood by neighborhood.

A lot of the doors are called "settings" and when you open one, you will find another and perhaps even another. Open away. You can always go back. Remember, your children are wandering around this "city" as they wish and it is very important you know something about the terrain and the potential hazards. Remember too that they may be accomplished travelers, able to cover a great deal of ground in a very short period of time.

Once you have a sense of the nature of the landscape you can begin to develop mental maps so that you and your children can explore it with safety and efficiency. You might find some murky alleyways in your explorations.

You don't need to walk down them, however, but it is just as well that you know they are there so that you can protect your less worldly and more vulnerable children.

NETIQUETTE

Some of our schools are accepting the challenge and teaching "netiquette" to their students—a set of social and ethical rules for the use of the Internet and electronic media.

Rules provide a set of boundaries, and if we stay within those boundaries, society tends to avoid a lot of the bumps and clashes that can make for insecurity and instability. We use knives, forks, and spoons to eat because it is more hygienic and we can avoid the spread of micro-organisms that cause disease. They keep us safe. We take turns with all sorts of things because it is a way in which we demonstrate our respect for other people and their rights. Taking turns minimizes the need to fight for our rights and so limits aggression. It keeps us safe.

If we stop and think about some seemingly odd social etiquette we can find its origins in actions to keep us safe. Men shaking hands was a way of demonstrating that neither had a weapon.

RULES THAT HELP SMOOTH THE WAY

Chat rooms, social media sites such as Facebook, and discussion boards can be great fun and highly informative. They can also be tricky and more than a little dangerous for an experienced user if discretion is not the order of the day. A few simple rules will keep youngsters safe.

Make sure they understand the privacy settings and set them for maximum privacy. Take the time to read the information on the web site thoroughly. An adult should be a part of the setting up of any chat room, discussion board, or social media site. Younger children—and some adults—are not clear about what is meant when posts can be shared, for example, not just with friends, but with friends of friends—in other words, with almost any and every one.

Impress on youngsters the need to keep personal details such as telephone numbers and addresses secret. They should never post a photo of themselves in circumstances that they would not be proud for their grandmother to see.

It is important to encourage young people to read what other people have to say. Just as in a face-to-face conversation we learn about other people and explore different points of view by listening carefully to them, we can do the same with online conversations.

Remember that typing in upper case is considered to be shouting

We need to warn them to look out for the trolls and the flamers. These are people who insert themselves into conversations with the sole purpose of causing trouble. They trade on their anonymity and will make provocative or insulting comments simply in order to get a reaction. Students should be told to either ignore them or exit the discussion.

> When your child is alone in his or her bedroom with a tablet or smartphone, how do you know that they are safe? How do you take the grown-up's role and monitor and control the sorts of things your child is accessing and the amount of time your child is spending online or playing games? That Internet-connected device is a doorway into the outside world. You monitor who has access to your child through the physical doorway of your home and you control where you allow your children to go when they walk out of that physical front door. How do you monitor their travels when they move in and out of the door within the Internet—a huge, exciting, rich, and potentially dangerous environment?

If anyone on line suggests meeting in person, make sure that youngsters know to immediately discuss this with an adult. It may be innocent. Perhaps a child has been talking to someone else of a similar age who enjoys the same pass times or hobby. But occasionally they are not so innocent.

There are many applications available that enable parents to use their own devices as a kind of remote for their children's devices. Parents can set up limits on the amount of time spent using the device as well as restrictions on the kinds of activities that are carried out. At the time of writing, the ITunes store has an app called ParentKit and the Google Play store has MMGuardian Parental Control. Windows 8 has parent-configurable "Family Safety" settings that allow a parent to set up a wide variety of limitations and controls on their children's access.

Of course, operating systems change and apps come and go, but all you need to do is search for "parental controls" with your search engine.

Without some sort of filtering on a child's mobile device, access to some disturbing places is scarily easy. Consider the teenage boy who was surfing through some gaming sites when he saw a link to something called "Farm Girls." He was a curious lad and thought he might see some pictures of pretty girls in denim with straw in their hair. Instead he was confronted by images of bestiality. It was only behavior over the following days that made his parents explore what had happened.

Many a child who watched and loved the movie "Babe" has been shocked by the images that appeared when they went to Google Images and searched for "babe." You try it. Our naïve youngsters hear terms on television, they overhear their parents' discussions, and they are eager to find out just what people are talking about. They search for images and then have to deal with what they find. Mostly they are too embarrassed to tell their parents what they have seen and so they have to process it alone.

It is a tragic fact that many of our young men have had some of their first sexual experiences mediated through the prism of online pornography. At a sensitive period in their lives, when they are just beginning to form the attitudes and values about sexuality that will guide them in later life, they are exposed to the norms of the pornography industry. They see the same scenarios enacted time and time again, and they come to believe that what they see must be normal.

WHERE TO BEGIN?

Today it is not enough to simply impose rules from above. The authority of the adult is changing, but it is not necessarily diminishing. The grown-ups still need to be in charge, but it is best if it is in a more consultative and involving fashion, where the kids are brought into the process. Here is an excellent opportunity to do a bit of deeper thinking and come to some mutually acceptable, understood, and negotiated rules.

If our goal is to encourage our young people to THINK more deeply about what they are doing with digital media and the World Wide Web, we need to start by inviting them to disengage from it all long enough to think about it. True, you could just come up with a set of rules and post them on the wall. Be prepared for resistance! Or you can work up a set of rules with your children and know that they had buy-in. You will still get resistance—kids will always pull at the traces—but you are standing on firmer ground when they helped to formulate the rules after having thought about the issues.

SMARTPHONES AND TABLETS

∼ A good discussion and thought starter might be to formulate together a set of acceptable, sociable behaviors around the use of mobile phones. Your circumstances will determine which rules are appropriate and in alignment with your values and way of life.

It is up to adults to establish a balance between what is best for a child and that child's right to privacy. This could be a fruitful topic for a parent and teacher evening at the school, with a focus of cyber safety.

School-age children might need rules about when their phones are turned off at night, and they probably need to be kept outside the bedroom to remove temptations. If you have a rule about no eating after the bedtime teeth cleaning routine, you wouldn't leave a block of chocolate on the bedside table. Having a parking place for phones that have been placed on silent during meal times could be a good idea too. Once the meal is over, the table cleared, the dishwasher stacked, then phones can be checked for incoming texts or messages. Similarly agreement needs to be reached about the status of phones when there is homework or study to be done in the evening or the weekend.

THE WIFI PASSWORD CAN BE EARNED BY COMPLETING CHORES AROUND THE HOUSE

Some parents have developed contracts with their children regarding the acceptable use of smartphones. A useful starting point might be to point out that the phone is paid for by the parent and this gives the parent certain rights—to know the password or unlock pattern of the phone, to have the final say about which apps can be downloaded, to be aware and to approve of all those who have access to the phone via phone calls, text messages, instant messaging, Skype calls, and the like. Just as parents control who enters the home through the front door or who may speak to their child on the landline phone, a similar gate-keeping role is needed to keep children safe in the electronic world.

Some parents may decide they require access to the contents of the phone from time to time. They may want to look through their child's contact list, their Facebook page posts, their messages, and the like.

This is a sensitive area and the degree of intrusion into the child's world will be dictated by the parents' attitudes toward privacy.

Privacy guidelines change as children become older. You may have no hesitation in going through a five-year-old's school bag, looking at all the notes and drawings. You may feel very differently about the book bag of a seventeen-year-old. Most parents would not hesitate to look through a six-year-old's diary, but the diary of a sixteen-year-old is a very different matter. You may never consider going through your teenager's bedroom when things seem to be going well, but if you suspect drug use or are worried about the psychological welfare of an adolescent, those privacy boundaries may shift.

For all of these reasons it is important that adults think carefully about the boundaries and limits they place on their children's use of electronic technology. If you decide to formulate a contract, do it in consultation with your child. Make the rules explicit but also allow some wriggle room should circumstances change. Every contract will be different and every contract needs to be the result of conversation and some focused deep thinking.

Talking, texting, or checking for updates on a phone when in the company of others can be an antisocial act because by doing so a person is turning their attention away from the people who are physically present. We teach our children it is impolite to whisper to one person in a group. We need to teach them that interacting with their phones is similar to whispering.

When we take our children out to dinner, or to visit grandparents, aunts, or uncles, on a train journey or just shopping at the local supermarket, an important part of the learning they do in that situation is the social learning. This is when children learn the appropriate use of language in different social situations. They learn how to interact successfully with people of different ages and with different interests and discover the consequences of using playground language with an elderly, perhaps very conservative relative. By watching their parents' behavior with grandparents they will learn how to deal compassionately with their own parents when they are aged.

Some schools have developed policies where mobile phones are simply banned from the premises. Parents may object to this on the grounds they want their child to be able to contact help in an emergency. Other schools have insisted that students leave their phones in their book bags or in their lockers. A cell phone is an expensive item and the school would need to ensure that there were places of safe keeping if the student is permitted to bring the phone into the school but not into the classroom.

If you allow or even encourage students to bring an Internet-connected device into the classroom it might be wise to insist that it always be placed on the top of the table or desk in full visibility. That way the teacher has some control over what is being done with the phone and is able to ensure that only school-related activities take place during classroom hours.

The principal of a secondary school in Western Australia attracted media interest when it was reported that she and her staff had banned the use of mobile phones during recess breaks at school. She noticed that during lunch and recess breaks girls were more likely to be found texting than engaging in face-to-face conversations with their friends. Believing that the development of the art of good conversation is a part of what school should be doing, the staff decided to implement a new phone policy, banning their use during recess times (http://www.abc.net.au/news/2013-10-28/hold-the-phone-perth-girls-school-bans-mobiles/5050214).

This is an example of the grown-ups taking charge for the benefit of the young people for whom they are responsible.

UNDERSTANDING THE SPREAD OF SOCIAL MEDIA

Social media are powerful and very enjoyable tools when we know how to use them. But just as a chain saw can remove a broken branch expeditiously, it can also remove a leg if used carelessly.

Social media are dramatic demonstrations of the added complexity that arises when we are no longer operating in a linear, sequential world. In the "old" literate world, before the Internet, before Twitter and Facebook, a child might tell a secret to a friend and ask that it not be passed on. Children being children, often it would be passed on and over time, a growing number of friends and acquaintances might come to know the secret. Children have sometimes been moved to a different school because this kind of gossip or rumor mongering has become hostile and bullying. A new school meant a new start.

We and our children need to understand the almost limitless speed and spread of anything that is committed to social media without privacy restrictions. The network is huge and information propagates through it virtually instantly. It is fairly safe to assume that what goes on the Internet stays on the Internet. If we do not place limits on who can access it, it is accessible to anyone who wants to look. That includes photographs, telephone numbers, addresses, and any other sort of identifying information.

We mentioned earlier the need to understand the privacy settings on social media sites. Both we and our children need to understand how to adjust these settings and recognize that by allowing "friends of friends" to view their posts there is almost no limit to how wide the audience might become.

🖎 Sit down with your child and a piece of paper and draw the "friends of friends" network. See how rapidly it grows to encompass a multitude of people that you don't know. This is a sobering exercise.

To test the efficacy of your social media settings ask someone else to log into that site and find out what they can see on yours. If that person is a "friend" and you have privacy settings that are intended to only allow friends to see your posts, that person should have access. If you can, ask someone who is not a "friend" to access your page so that you can assure yourself that your posts are not being displayed.

It has become a popular tactic for a class to put a post on Facebook with the request that people share it after commenting what part of the world they are in. On the January 21, 2016, a class at a school in Limerick, Ireland, created such a post with no privacy restrictions. By February 13—twenty-three days later—the post had been shared 164,000 times.

One mother recently engaged in a misadventure trying to demonstrate to her daughter how far a photo could spread. She posted a photo of her daughter and asked people to "like" it in order to demonstrate through the number of "likes" how fast a post could propagate, not understanding the privacy settings made her prey to an ever-growing number of dubious responders. The abuse that was directed at her and her daughter as a result of that post was a harsh way to learn about privacy settings.

It is important to understand the longevity of everything put on a social media site, and its reach. It is wise never to write anything that you wouldn't be prepared to say in public, to never post anything that might eventually be embarrassing. There are always personal message options for the things you might want to share only with a single individual. Make sure your children know how to use them.

Most parents are diligent about teaching their children how to be safe in public. They explain why they should never accept a car ride from a stranger, that they should avoid walking in isolated places alone, and that they should always try and have a buddy with them when doing anything potentially dangerous such as swimming in the ocean. We need to be equally as diligent about teaching them how to be safe in cyberspace as we are in physical space.

Once upon a time we took photographs of each other, took them along to a store to be processed, collected the negatives and the finished photos—the only copies there were—and took them home to sift through and then put in a box or an album. When great aunts or cousins came to visit, the photos might be taken out.

What happens today? Young people have their phones with them constantly and their phones are also powerful cameras. At any moment, perhaps when carried away by the fun or peer pressures of the moment, or maybe by alcohol, photos can be taken and then shared on social networks between friends, friends of friends, and then half the world. There is no time for judgment, it is all so instantaneous. Because the photo is of you doesn't mean you will have any control over who might see it. Do you really want grandma to see you like that? Or, five years later, when you are applying for a job and your prospective employer Googles your name, do you want him to see that photo?

Do your children understand the implications down the track of these photos? And if they don't, who will teach them? Are you aware that you can have a setting on your social media site that will require your permission before anyone can attach your name to any photo placed on the web? If your children don't know this, who will teach them? Even if a photo is deleted from a social media account, you cannot delete it from the computer of someone who may have chosen to download that photo.

> We need to have these thoughtful conversations with our children. We need to make the time and space for them to disconnect, move out of the shallows, and think about what they are doing in greater depth.

The immediacy of social media encourages rapid fire and often thoughtless action. The Internet is a world of all-at-onceness. The old restrictions of time and space have gone. You can't unsend an instant message. It arrives almost at the same time as you send it, to anywhere in the world. After hitting the send button that launches an unkind comment you can't phone up and say

"Hey, I'm sorry. You will getting a message soon and I was really thoughtless when I sent it. I would rather you just threw it away without reading it." The message arrived when you sent it.

We need to help our children disentangle themselves so that they can slow the process down and think.

Not everyone spends the same amount of time interacting on social media. Many youngsters carry their smartphone with them almost everywhere they go. They will have alerts that tell them when a friend has posted and will check it out immediately. Others may only look in once a day, others quite rarely.

Adolescents can carry their hearts on their sleeves and quite often gain a sense of relief sharing strong feelings—both positive and negative—with their friends. They will write a post on social media and then wait for the responses of their friends, anticipating that they will share in their joys and support them when they feel bad. It can be very disconcerting for a teenager to find that their best friends have not responded at all, and often this is misconstrued as them not caring, when in fact they may not have read the post.

⇝ Encourage youngsters to slow down, and disconnect from the to and fro of the medium for a while in order to think more deeply about why their friend has not responded. Social media encourages impulsive reactions because everything is instantaneous. Your message goes out in a fraction of a second and if nothing comes back as quickly there is a temptation to put out another message and another.

Online conversations can get caught up very easily in this kind of misunderstanding. A girl and boy are chatting online. The boy asks the girl if she really cares for him. It took some courage for him to ask and he is breathlessly awaiting a response. None comes. What he doesn't know is that in the girl's room the cat has just jumped up on her desk and knocked over her glass of orange juice all over her just completed and printed homework. She has leapt to her feet, hasn't read his last message, and is busily trying to clean up the mess before it drips on the carpet and makes a stain.

So the boy waits, and waits, and hearing nothing back in convinced he has made a false move. He shuts down the chat and mooches off to watch television. The next morning at school he avoids the girl because he is embarrassed that he has revealed too much of himself. The girl cannot understand why the boy who was perfectly friendly with her yesterday is suddenly avoiding her. And so it goes.

Once you begin to use a social media site it is very easy to get sucked into long discussions about all sorts of interesting and contentious issues. Someone makes a comment that you disagree with, you add your comment, and it's off! While these discussions can often be valuable and explore new ideas and varying points of view, they can also often wander off in unanticipated directions and even become abusive.

Some people take advantage of their anonymity and make claims that are untrue. Others pretend to be experts in things about which they know little. There are also the "trolls" and "flamers" whose only purpose is to inflame discussions or to infiltrate for less than honest purposes. They inject inflammatory comments and then sit back and watch the damage they have caused.

Our young people need to be explicitly aware of all these things and if we don't teach them, who will? They need to know when to exit from an online discussion thread and when to check the veracity of claims and quotations. They also need to understand that some people just like to cause trouble on line. When they know this and can filter what they read through the lense of these understandings they can make the most of social media in relative safety. If we don't teach them, they will learn through trial and error or from their friends. These friends are also learning by trial and error, and all without the experience and wisdom that only comes through having lived a lot more years.

Let's make time to talk with our kids about social media, about the pitfalls and misunderstandings that it makes possible as well as its advantages. We can encourage them to *disconnect and talk, to think more deeply* about what may have just happened, rather than remaining entangled in the web. This is another example of how important it is for our kids to disentangle themselves from the constant business in the shallows and move into the deep end where they can think at length and in depth about what is going on.

THOUGHTFUL EMAIL USE

Many children and almost all young adults have email accounts, although the evidence seems to be that they are using them less in favor of private messaging within social media sites.

It is important in an email to give the message a short, but descriptive subject. Why? Your children may come up with some great explanations if they are given the time to think about this question. Even though the email can be sent without a subject, most email programs will prompt for one. Emails sent by one person should never be forwarded without the original sender's permission. Children can think about this by comparing the forwarding of an email to the lending of a game or a piece of clothing to a third person without gaining the owner's permission first. Nothing is more infuriating than finding your own email grinding away as it tries to download a very large file. Make sure children understand that it is considerate to ask permission of the recipient before sending a large file. Better still, learn how to use a Dropbox. You can find information about Dropbox at www.dropbox.com.

THE VIRAL EMAIL

This new world of "all-at-onceness" and "anywhere-can-be-everywhere" means that emails can go viral. We use this word to describe the process because it is like an infection. One person passes it on to another and they pass it on to their friends who in turn pass it on, and pretty soon you have an epidemic. Like most epidemics, we usually have no idea who started it. We have no information that enables us to judge the reliability of the viral email by means of our knowledge of the reliability of its author.

IS IT TRUE?

Do you sometimes find emails in your inbox or posts on your social media page that make you gasp with amazement that something so terrible could actually be true? Are you disturbed to discover that your worst fears are supported and that there is, in fact, a giant conspiracy operating? Do you wonder why the medical profession isn't using the new wonder bean that cures everything from gout to cataracts? Or are you just sleeping less soundly at night because someone has predicted the end of the world in the next ten years?

These emails and posts are often the result of well-meaning friends reposting something they came across on the Internet. They repost it to their friends, their friends repost it to their friends, and on and on—suddenly it's gone viral because we were all vectors for infection!

These emails are often filled with what looks like factual information and data—quotes, descriptions of events, sentences from press releases, tables, and statistics. As Abraham Lincoln once said, "You can't trust everything you read on the Internet." We remember being taught at school to go back to primary sources and documents whenever possible. And why is this? Because it is so very easy to completely distort the message if you change the context.

Let's take an actual case. In mid-2012 the author and television presenter Clive James was interviewed by Radio 4 in London and in the course of the interview he mused on his own mortality and the fact that he was a lot closer to the end than to the beginning. This interview with its nuances, tones of voice, pauses, laughs, and the like was then taken up by a print journalist from the *Daily Mirror* and, without all these subtleties, his written article looked as though James was teetering on the edge of the grave. James was highly irritated by the rumors of his imminent death that this article sparked.

LOOK OUT FOR URBAN MYTHS

Urban myths are stories that have somehow become rooted in popular culture or belief without any foundation in fact. An early example is the panic in 1938 caused by the radio play *The War of the Worlds* narrated by Orson Wells. It began with an apparent news broadcast describing the arrival on earth of Martian space ships. Adding to the problem is the proliferation of satirical and fake news sites.

We need to encourage young people to question what they read and hear, to help them drill through the surface layers and get to the sources. One very useful web site to help with this task is www.snopes.com. Here you can type in the latest rumor or viral "fact" and begin to test its veracity and reliability. Snopes will provide information about where it came from and what other information is available to help us decide if it is "true," "false," or "undecided."

Skilled thinkers ask questions and take in data through all their senses and from all their sources. The Internet serves the rumor mill like nothing ever has before. Thinking is the tool that can apply a vaccine to control viral emails. We need to remember to think before hitting the "send" button.

The grade 7 English Language Arts: Reading Informational Text standard states that students should be able to

> Trace and evaluate the argument and specific claims in a text, assessing whether the reasoning is sound and the evidence is relevant and sufficient to support the claims. (CCS, 2009, ELA-LITERACY.RI.7.8)

GOOGLE AND ALL THE "STUFF"

There is more information available to us now than there has ever been. Once upon a time if we wanted to know where Christopher Columbus was born, we would need to go to our local library and hunt through the history section. It was a straightforward, linear process. Once we got to the library we would look through the sequentially ordered catalogue and then walk the aisles of books looking for the Dewey reference number.

Today we have Professor Google and he can provide us with an avalanche of information in a split second without having to leave the table. If you get an ache in your knee, Dr Google may be your first port of call. You want to know what is in the new medication the doctor has prescribed and does it have any side effects that he hasn't warned about. Where do you go? You can go to your ever ready, twenty-four-hour pharmacist, Dr Google. Specialists in all walks of life are confronted more and more frequently by clients with printouts from web sites telling how they might do their jobs better.

Google is the great homework helper too. Do our students really know how to use Google when they are studying, doing homework, or researching for school projects? Who is teaching them? Do they understand that there is a huge difference between the medical information they will get from the Mayo Clinic web site and from "ICanFixIt.com?"

What does it mean to know how to search for, to evaluate, and to analyze online information? It doesn't mean accepting at first glance whatever we read on a computer or tablet screen when it pops up as a result of a Google search. The one thing we are no longer short of is information.

FINDING SAFE INFORMATION

> It ain't what you don't know that gets you into trouble. It's what you know for sure that just ain't so.
>
> —Mark Twain

We want our kids to access the information and ideas out there, but we also want them to be discriminating and able to sort the wheat from the chaff. How do we do this?

➥ Yet again it will require our students to stop and think for a bit before they do anything else.

What Are You Looking For?

Spending a little time refining the search terms before typing them into a search engine will not only help your students to sharpen their own understandings about what they need to know, it will also help ensure that relevant material is obtained.

Where Should You Look?

For younger children it is a good idea to bookmark specific web sites suitable for children. Lists of these sites can be found if you search for "web sites suitable for children" and one useful list created by school librarians is found at http://www.sldirectory.com/libsf/resf/kidsafe.html.

Many of these lists are ephemeral, and they grow, change, and sometimes disappear over time. That's the nature of the Internet. But you can always do your own search.

You can find Wikipedia sites that are suitable for kids if you use http://www.wikiforkids.ws/ and http://www.safesearchkids.com/ gives you access to safe sites and image downloads.

http://scholar.google.com is a powerful database of scholarly articles that can provide a rich and reliable resource for older students.

How Up to Date is the Information?

At the top of your search engine you will find a set of search tools that enable you to select the time span you want to cover. Do you want very recent information, or are you looking for information that is from a particular date or time period in the past?

Do You Want Information Relevant to Your Country or to the Entire World?

Check out the search tools for this too.

Is the Source Reliable?

⌒ This is another important time to stop and think more deeply. If I want some information and advice about sailing I will turn to someone who knows something about the subject. I am more inclined to trust the information about the treatment of my shattered shoulder after falling off my bike when I speak with an orthopedic doctor than when I talk to an ear, nose, and throat specialist.

Similarly it is important to look at the source of the information we gain from the Internet. This isn't always easy. We can safeguard younger children by directing them to specific, trustworthy, and reliable web sites. Older students want to do their own research and the charlatans are sometimes hard to identify. When an adult reads something and thinks "that just doesn't seem right," that is a judgment made after comparing this information with other information gleaned over years of reading, listening, watching, and generally amassing life experience. A sixteen-year-old has very little life experience.

HOW DO WE ACCOMMODATE THIS LACK OF EXPERIENCE?

Teach your students to pause and dig a little deeper into the source of the information they uncover in their research, to think about the *who* as well as the *what*. Help them understand that it is far better to learn from one or two reliable sources than to amass doubtful material from eight or ten.

BE MORE THAN JUST A COLLECTOR

Because information can be so readily harvested we must guard against the temptation to become simply a curator of information. In the early days of photocopiers people would say in jest that if an article had been copied and filed, it had been as good as read. Our filing cabinets filled up with things we had curated rather than read, in the usually vain hope that we would "come back to it later." Every now and then we would cull these collections and hopefully recycle the wasted paper and articles that had lost their relevance with the passage of time.

Today it is so much easier to collect information electronically because there are no drawers to be filled, no shelves to be stuffed with the results of our searches. We cut, we clip, we save, and we post. We collect. We curate.

But we must also teach our children—and perhaps ourselves—how to be selective, analytical, and evaluative and how to synthesize the valuable information Google has provided.

The Common Core State Standards include in the grade 6 Writing standards the goal that students should be able to

> Gather relevant information from multiple print and digital sources; assess the credibility of each source and quote or paraphrase the data and conclusions of others while avoiding plagiarism and providing basic bibliographic information for sources. (CCS, 2009, ELA-LITERACY.W.6.8)

It is not enough for them to be curators at a time when it is easier than ever to be one. They must be able to make reasoned judgments about what is and is not relevant and then transform it into their own words, make it their own. Collect it, think deeply about it, use it, or file it away for future use.

TEACHING WHAT WE CAN NOT GOOGLE

Ewan McIntosh is a teacher, and expert in digital media in business and in education. He is regarded as one of Europe's foremost experts in digital media for public services. At a recent conference he said that what we should be teaching are the things that are NOT Googleable.

In other words, what we should be teaching our children is how to think about the information that is so readily accessible. Rather than spending time teaching them the names of the Presidents of the United States, the kings and queens of England, or the dates of famous battles, we should be teaching them how to think about these things, how to analyze, how to compare, how to predict, and how to look at the past and interpret the present.

It's not that facts and information are unimportant. They are both inevitable and crucial. Let's use an analogy—a flour mill. A flour mill takes in grain, feeds it through a milling process, and produces flour. The process of milling cannot take place without the grain. Teaching our children how to think is analogous to the grinding process, making them able to mill the facts effectively and efficiently, to produce quality end products, namely worthwhile, well-judged, reasonable, creative thoughts. You can't grind flour without grain, and you can't think without information to think about.

The facts we teach our children are all grist to the mill. Quality flour depends on quality grain and so quality thinking needs to grow out of quality information. But the grain and the information are not ends in themselves. Knowing names and dates, being able to replicate a formula or the steps in a process are not worthwhile ends in themselves. They need to be "milled" by the mind. They need to be thought about.

At school our children are taught a lot of "stuff." Every subject has its own content. In some subjects, mathematics for example, we also teach children a large number of routines where they feed in the numbers, turn the crank, and pump out an answer. As long as children know the "stuff" and can perform the routines, they tend to do very well at school. But the rapid changes in the world make it very difficult to determine exactly what "stuff" and which routines are essential, hence all the discussions and disputes about what should be included in a common curriculum.

There was a time when any course in senior mathematics would have included training in how to use logarithms and, later, a slide rule. The slide rule became a kind of analog, mechanical computer and the mainstay of any relatively complex mathematical calculations. Engineers and scientists couldn't operate without one. By the late 1970s the electronic scientific calculator made the slide rule obsolete. Teaching the operations of the slide rule will no longer be found in any twenty-first-century curriculum and it would be considered the height of folly to continue to teach something that is no longer useful.

How many other items in the curriculum are being retained simply because we have always done it this way? When was the last time you needed to work something out by long division, without a calculator? When did you last find the knowledge of the correct sequence of the kings of England to be significant, or the names of the countries in Africa? Is it more important to know the names of the river systems, the capital cities of each state, or the stages of mitosis in a plant cell?

There is so much "stuff" that we could be teaching, but not enough time for it all. And so we make decisions to include some and leave other things out. What is important knowledge for a child growing up in a rural, agricultural setting is far different from that needed by a city child. A child living by the ocean would find very different areas of knowledge relevant than would a child from an arid, desert region. It all depends.

Consider the teacher, a city boy, who was teaching in a small rural school in a sheep grazing area. Not known for his artistic abilities he spent an entire lunch time drawing a sheep on the chalkboard in preparation for his unit on the wool industry. After forty minutes of concentrated effort he stood back and admired his work. Not bad. He then pulled down the map of the world that was affixed above the board, and covered his drawing.

When the children came into the classroom after lunch playtime, he settled them down and with considerable fanfare and the question "Who can tell me what this is?" he retracted the map and revealed his drawing. The room was silent and some of the children's faces showed distinct puzzlement. He wondered to himself if his drawing could really be that bad. Eventually one boy tentatively raised his hand. "I'm not sure, sir, but is it a Border Leicester/ Southdown cross?" Clearly the curriculum content for this group of children would have to change from the one this city-bred teacher had devised.

One of the skills we learned in the 1990s was how to clean a mouse. We had ergonomic mice, trackball mice, mice with scrolling dials, and wireless mice. Today's young people live in a world of touch screens. Who needs a mouse? Recall the old spirit duplicators or mimeograph machines and the purple fingers that seemed an inevitable consequence of their use. Generations of school children have held the freshly made copies to their noses and smelled the aroma of the newly minted work sheet. All we need today is the ability to activate the "print" button on the computer, tablet, or smartphone screen and one or multiple copies of documents and photographs begin to appear. Did you lose a button from your favorite shirt? Soon the 3D printer in the study will be able to create one for you in a matter of seconds.

> The world is changing fast and the skills we need are changing with it. It is good to know that there is one skill that is not changing, one that was critical in the past, is needed to day and will be essential for success in whatever the future brings us. That is, the ability to think. Our focus as educators—either as teachers or parents—should be firmly on teaching our kids how to think about the massive amount of ever-changing "stuff" there is out there to be thought about.

WHAT WOULD SOCRATES HAVE SAID?

Socrates, in the Phaedrus, lamented the invention of writing and reading. He feared that they would replace the oral culture by which knowledge and wisdom had been passed down in previous generations. Human memory would cease to be of value and the young would become progressively more ignorant as they relied more and more on written texts rather than the memorization of information. Imagine his discomfort if he had been aware of the immenseness of the Internet and the knowledge contained within it.

Plato gives the following words to Socrates as he discusses the written word with Phaedrus:

> I cannot help feeling, Phaedrus, that writing is unfortunately like painting; for the creations of the painter have the attitude of life, and yet if you ask them a question they preserve a solemn silence. And the same may be said of speeches. You would imagine that they had intelligence, but if you want to know anything and put a question to one of them, the speaker always gives one unvarying answer. And when they have been once written down they are tumbled about anywhere among those who may or may not understand them, and know not to whom they should reply, to whom not: and, if they are maltreated or abused, they have no parent to protect them; and they cannot protect or defend themselves.

His fears went deeper than simply his concerns about the loss of the ability to remember by rote. He valued the principles of Socratic argument, encouraging ongoing questioning and reformulation of thoughts. Socrates' misgivings can be applied equally well to the information found on the Internet when our young people think that because they found it on the Internet it must be true. *They need to interrogate the information, they need to think in depth about it.*

Like most assessments of new technology, Socrates' analysis was partly right and partly wrong. He was right in that the written word does suppress our need for memory. We all carry notebooks, physical or electronic, to jot down information we intend for later. But without the writings of Plato we would know nothing about Socrates and his ideas today. Writing lasts generations, long beyond the ability of storytellers to remember the details. The sheer quantity of knowledge and ideas available to us today is beyond anything Socrates could have imagined. We may not need to know what is going on in Athens, but we need to be aware of the events in London, Beijing, Pyongyang, Damascus, and Washington.

Socrates was thinking of the life he was living at the time. He did not recognize that important developments like writing will evolve and actually change the fabric of the future. We have to be aware of this capacity to change society when we consider the digital revolution. We have to guide our children through the difficulties of an emerging technology while remaining aware that this technology will influence and change every part of the workplaces our adult children will occupy.

GOOGLE GOBBLEDYGOOK

While engaged in a recent Facebook discussion around gun violence in the United Kingdom the following newspaper reports were cited in support of different points of view. Other opinion sources were also provided, some in enthusiastic support of the current limitations on the use of guns by police in the United Kingdom and others eager for a police force armed as it is in the United States.

> Culture of violence: Gun crime goes up by 89% in a decade: *Daily Mail*
> Police winning battle against inner city gun crime: *The Independent*

It would have been easy to come away from that discussion either dismayed or vindicated in one's own opinion, depending on which links you chose to follow and which you chose to believe. For a young person attempting to develop an opinion based on fact, the problems are significant.

It is important to notice when the two articles were published. The Daily Mail article came out in 2009 and The Independent article was published four years later in 2013. A lot can change in four years. It is also important to do a little more research and determine if these reports are painting a nation-wide picture or only a picture of events in a particularly difficult inner suburban area. Some deeper digging would reveal that some of the opinion pieces came from online sites with a vested interest in one position or the other. Data can be "cherry picked" to support almost any point of view.

Following this online argument was a disheartening experience because it could be seen how feelings were being aroused and how each participant was Googling to find something, anything to support their own point of view. There was very little, if any, evidence of careful discrimination in the use of online "authorities."

This is what Sugata Mitra meant when he described the three tasks of twenty-first-century education as the teaching of reading comprehension, the ability to search for, retrieve, and analyze information, and what he calls "a rational system of belief." Increasingly young people are basing their systems of belief on what they and their peers learn on the Internet. We need to ensure that they have the skills not simply to retrieve information, but then to analyze it and question its rational foundations.

In other words, and in Socrates-imputed language, we need to make sure we do not place our young people in the dangerous situation where things:

> have been once written down they are tumbled about anywhere among those who may or may not understand them, and know not to whom they should reply, to whom not: and, if they are maltreated or abused, they have no parent to protect them; and they cannot protect or defend themselves.

As the adults in society we must ensure that we give our young people the tools they need to protect and defend themselves from the torrent of information that flows into their minds, unfiltered, from the Internet.

They must learn how to stop collecting and start connecting.

👉 We help our children distinguish between Google information and gobbledygook by teaching them how to think more deeply and ask questions like these:

- Why should I believe this?
- Is the writer an authority?
- Does the writer have any ulterior motives?
- Do other reputable sources verify this material?
- Is the material up to date?
- Can I verify the truth of the statements via another source?

EVEN WHEN WE SLEEP

William Hermanns (1895–1990), a German sociologist and antiwar poet, fled Germany in 1934 and in 1937 he was allowed entrance into the United States. In 1946 he was appointed Professor of German Language and Literature at San Jose State College (now University) to serve until 1965, when he became emeritus professor. From 1973 to 1984 he was a visiting scholar in the Hoover Institution for War, Revolution and Peace at Stanford University. His friendship with Albert Einstein and conversations he had with him both before and after the war are described in his book *Einstein and the Poet: In Search of Cosmic Man*.

He recounts one conversation that is relevant to our considerations in which Einstein said:

> Knowledge is necessary, too. An intuitive child couldn't accomplish anything without some knowledge. There will come a point in everyone's life, however where only intuition can make the leap ahead, without ever knowing precisely how. One can never know why but one must accept intuition as a fact.

We all have bright ideas that seem to spring out of thin air. We have those "aha" moments when something previously obscure and indistinct becomes suddenly clear. At other times we unexpectedly understand a connection between things that we hadn't been aware of previously. The subconscious mind is working even when we are asleep and many people will tell you of occasions when a problem that seemed insoluble when they went to bed is resolved the next morning with little effort after a good night's sleep. What is going on?

Functional magnetic resonance imaging has shown us that our brains do not go into suspended animation when we sleep. They continue to process things even when we are unaware of it. But for our brains to process, they must have some raw material and this is where information and experience are important.

It may not seem important to remember the dates when events happened simply for the sake of remembering them, but if we do remember these dates then our brains have the opportunity to uncover links between the different things that happened at different times. Understanding how a sequence of events led to a particular conclusion is entirely dependent on knowing the sequence of events.

We should not rely on having a "google memory." Our brains need information to process. When we think, we think about something, and that something is the information we have amassed throughout our lives. It isn't enough to leave it all to Google. We need to have a lot of it in our memories if we are going to have a lot to think about.

KEY IDEAS IN THIS CHAPTER

- Don't be afraid to explore and play with digital devices, apps, and medium. That's the best way to learn.
- Have some clear safety rules:
  o Understand and use the privacy settings.
  o Never reveal personal details on social media sites.
  o Pay attention to what other people are saying online.
  o Watch out for trolls.
- Parents and teachers should make use of filtering programs to block inappropriate web sites and consider set time limits.
- Encourage youngsters to think by mutually deciding on rules.
- Social media can spread things rapidly and this can be powerful and dangerous.
- What you put on social media stays there—permanently.
- The immediacy of the digital world can lead to unrealistic expectations.
- There are generally accepted rules about email use.
- Web sites like www.snopes.com can help sift rumor from fact, and other sites provide forums for safe searching.
- Google is a great way to collect dots. Thoughtful people need to know how to connect dots.
- The three Rs of twenty-first-century learning are reading comprehension, the ability to search for, retrieve, and analyze information, and the ability to assess the veracity and value of that information.
- Our children need to both know and remember information if they are to be able to think effectively and critically.

DISCUSSION

- How would you go about determining a set of appropriate rules for device usage in your school/classroom/home?
- List some of the major considerations and road blocks.
- Describe how you would monitor the success of your rules. What adaptations might become necessary?
- Have you come across any "urban myths?" What might be some of the steps for verification?

Chapter Twelve

Metacognition

What We Do When We Think in the Deep End

We are awash with information and the tricky thing is to know what to do with it all. Never before in the history of the human race has the average person had access to as much information as we have today. Within a matter of moments we can know the population of Kurdistan, the main exports of Belgium, and the exact wording of the United Nations Declaration on the Rights of the Child. We can take a guided tour of the Louvre Museum and see the works of Picasso from his boyhood into old age. We can discover the writer of a few lines of poetry remembered from years ago, and we can read a list of every significant newspaper article written by a favorite correspondent.

With no entry requirements, no fees, no complex registration process, and no need to leave our living rooms, we can complete Harvard University's "Intensive Introduction to Computer Science" or study "China: Traditions and Transformations." There is no limit to the "stuff" we can learn. Is it any wonder that education systems all over the world constantly squabble and disagree about what should be included in any core curriculum?

Working with groups in both Australia and the USA we have asked a similar question. "What would you like students to have retained five years after they leave school?" We have found a remarkable agreement among teachers, administrators, employers, parents, and senior citizens. Not once has anyone mentioned they want them know a particular set of dates, or be able to recite the periodic table, the names of explorers in the New World. In fact they don't even consider the "stuff" or the routines.

What they want is for young people to have become independent learners, good team members, and cooperative and responsible citizens. They want them to be able to find their way in the world, to solve problems, and to persist at tasks until they reach completion. They want them to be resilient, compassionate, and thoughtful. One ability permeates many of the things they hope for—the ability to think flexibly, creatively, effectively, and efficiently. They also want their children to be able to reason logically, to analyze and judge the validity of information, and to solve problems.

Increasingly we read that employers are not simply looking for people who know the "stuff" required to do the job. They want people who can think effectively, flexibly, and creatively, who can communicate their ideas, and who can work well with others. If they have these qualities, employers know their employees will be able to deal with the "stuff," even when the "stuff" changes from week to week, year to year.

But no matter how well they know the "stuff," if they cannot think and problem-solve, if they cannot work flexibly and creatively with their fellow workers, they will soon become a liability rather than an asset.

In the United States and in Australia we are watching the workforce changing as some industries close down and others open up. When a major automobile production plant closed recently, hundreds of employees, many of whom had worked for the same company for decades, found themselves unemployed, and in their fifties. Having the skills involved in building a car is only of very limited value in finding future work if that is all you know how to do.

The most successful person is the one who has sufficient flexibility to think about how to transfer those skills to a new work environment. Transference of skills, be they manual or intellectual, depends on our ability to think about the old skills, understand the demands of the new tasks, and exercise sufficient understanding and flexibility to adapt and modify those skills to suit the new demands.

Successful transition into a new industry rarely depends being able to tighten widgets, assemble a specific product, operate an accounting software program, carry out a forensic process in a laboratory, or write a review of new four-wheel-drive vehicle. The motoring writer who finds himself moved to a division of the newspaper that reports on politics had better be able to adapt, to learn quickly from those around him, to assess his new situation and its demands and be able to make sound decisions based on his capacity to think flexibly, creatively, and to work effectively with others.

At school we expend a great deal of time and energy teaching our young people information and how to perform routines. These things only become useful in their lives when youngsters are able to transfer their new learnings to the solving of the real problems they will encounter in their lives. There is not much point in learning about fractions if, when faced with the task of understanding how a budget has been allocated, an individual isn't able to transfer that school knowledge to the problem at hand.

> It is revealing to note that students in the United States have regularly performed better on TIMSS assessments than they have on PISA. The major difference between these two forms of testing is that TIMSS measures the retention of the taught curriculum and PISA measures the ability to apply it in novel situations.

Getting ten sums correct out of ten doesn't mean the child understands how to apply fractions. That application requires a level of thinking that goes well beyond the simple ability to perform mathematical routines. It requires the ability to understand the nature of the problem and then transfer knowledge from one context into a new one.

THE INTERNET GIVES US SO MUCH "STUFF" TO THINK ABOUT

How much time and energy do we invest in teaching our children how to think? In other words, as we are teaching them at home and at school, are we also making sure that our children are explicitly aware of how they are learning? Do they understand the tool that is the most important tool they will ever have, far more powerful than a slide rule, a computer, a smartphone, or an iPad—their brains? Nothing is learned without the brain and without thought. It is the tool of learning.

If we do not understand the nature of the tools we use, we will never learn to use them effectively. The child who hammers a nail into a piece of wood in a clumsy and inefficient manner may continue to do so unless an adult explains that she should never "choke" the hammer, that she should hold it well away from its head and let the weight of the head and the momentum of its motion do the hard work. Once she understands how the tool works best, she will be able to use it more effectively. When she understands that there are different kinds of hammers for different tasks, a carpenter's hammer, a geologist's hammer, an upholstery hammer, a mallet, or a jack hammer, she will be able to choose the right tool for the task. So it is with thinking—select the correct tool for the task and use it effectively.

If we teach our children how to think well we will have given them the most transferable skill that will ever be available to them. It will serve them at school, regardless of the content of what is taught. It will serve them in society regardless of the nature of that society and the speed with which it morphs and changes. And it will serve them in their adult lives as they negotiate their work and their domestic lives. It will give them the tools to resolve problems they haven't ever encountered before.

THINKING METACOGNITIVELY—IN THE DEEP END

Perhaps the deepest kind of thinking we can do is when we think about our own thinking. We are not thinking simply about the content of our thinking. We are thinking about the *processes* of thinking. Only when we understand HOW we think, can we be in control of our thinking and use it most effectively.

Thinking is something that we do constantly, but most of the time we do it almost without being aware of what we are doing. We constantly make decisions, express opinions, analyze and evaluate things, and it is only when someone asks us "Why did you say that?" that we become conscious of our thinking, and often we struggle to give an answer. Young children seem to have a stock reply to this kind of question. How many times do you hear a youngster respond with the one word "because" when asked why he thinks a particular way about something? This kind of response reveals that our children are not spontaneously inclined to focus on their thinking.

Thinking is a tool they use every day but they do not tend to consider how the tool works and nor do they seek to improve their technique, unless we provide them with guidance. For most children, and for many adults, thinking just "happens." Thinking is the most important tool we have for dealing with a very problematic world and we need to make sure we help our children use this tool as effectively as possible.

This is where we need to make sure that our children have the words available to talk about their thinking and then we must help them to think constructively about their own thinking. Behind the answer "because" lies the problem of vocabulary. We can only talk about the things for which we have the words. In every sphere of human activity, in every hobby, every profession, every daily activity, there is a specific vocabulary that we must learn in order to become proficient. The chemist needs to learn the words for the chemicals, the chemical reactions, and the apparatus she uses, the teacher knows the vocabulary of curriculum and pedagogy, and the cook knows the difference between beating, folding, and creaming. So too the thinker needs to know the vocabulary of thinking, the difference between comparing and contrasting, the ways in which to analyze and evaluate, and what it means to sequence and to prioritize.

When we are consciously aware of our thinking and when we have the vocabulary necessary to speak about how we are thinking, then we are thinking metacognitively. Metacognitive thinking is the key to successful thinking.

Metacognition is not a process that has been explicitly taught until quite recently. In the past individuals have worked out ways to monitor their own thinking, but often not in any organized way. Recently psychologists and educators have begun to study cognitive processes and to monitor brain activity, so that much more is known about how people think and how an individual's thinking can be improved. Adults can help children (and themselves) gain an understanding by questioning the thought process.

Arthur Costa and Bena Kallick in their book *Leading and Learning with Habits of Mind* describe four aspects of metacognitive thinking (Costa and Kallick, 2008):

1. *Understanding that you are thinking*—this means being aware that you are using your mind for some well-defined purpose. This includes recognizing the type of thinking you are using and your disposition toward the thinking task. For example, I might be aware that I am *making judgments* between two different courses of action in the future and I am *seeking data* and taking into account my own and other's *past experiences*.
2. *Monitor your thinking*—this involves checking that your thought processes are reasonable and moving you toward your purpose.
3. *Evaluate your thinking*—asking yourself if the results of your thinking are reasonable and consistent with what you already know.
4. *Regulating your thinking*—this is a kind of debriefing of the thinking process and is the key to improving thinking in the future. You ask yourself if, when faced with a similar problem in the future, you would proceed in a similar way or perhaps do some things differently.

➤ Adults can guide children's thinking by questioning it—asking them to tell you what is going on in their mind.

To promote awareness and understanding of thinking you might ask, "How did you figure that out?" or "What made you think of that?" or "How did you know that?"

To encourage monitoring of thinking you might ask questions such as "What are you trying to achieve?" "What was your intention or goal?" "How were you proceeding?" "Were you using the best thinking tools?" and "Was your attitude up to the task?"

We can help them evaluate their thinking by asking questions like "Were you satisfied with the outcome of your thinking?" and "Does that seem right given everything else you know?"

Finally, you can help them to debrief and regulate their future thinking by asking, "Would different thinking help next time?" and "If faced with a similar situation would you go about it in the same way?"

Remember that you are not asking these questions just to get an answer. There is a much more important purpose—you want to stimulate reflection. Don't accept quick or glib answers. Probe for more depth, encourage thinking beyond the obvious, and get below the surface and the superficial.

Deciding what to cook for dinner is a thinking task and we do it without really questioning ourselves about *how* we came to the decision. If we stop for a moment and consider what kinds of thinking we needed to engage in order to make that decision, we find quite an array.

First we needed to interrogate our own desires and preferences—what foods appeal to me today? Am I in the mood for lots of vegetables, a salad, or do I want to get my teeth into some red meat? Then we need to consider our finances and determine if there is enough money in the housekeeping budget this week to purchase what is wanted. A survey of the fridge and the pantry will reveal what might need to be purchased and a consideration of the day's obligations will reveal if there will be enough time to go shopping. If there are time pressures we may need to evaluate what can be postponed to another day and what is urgent and must be completed today. Once the decisions have been made and the requirements obtained there is some sequencing that needs to be done—what do I prepare first, and how do I make sure everything arrives at the table at the same time, cooked and still hot?

There are a large number of thinking tools used in this apparently simple daily task—surveying, comparing, sequencing, arranging, evaluating, and so on. For an experienced house keeper it comes easily but for a young parent, dealing with a spouse, a job, and maybe a child, things may not run as smoothly and the meat might arrive at the table cooked while the potatoes are still boiling on the stove and there is no mustard in the refrigerator.

When faced with a new, complex task or trying to resolve an unfamiliar problem we need to be able to break down the thinking part of the task, understand how we are thinking, and adjust as needed. The young parent would be greatly helped by paying attention to the sequencing part of his evening meal routine if that is where things were going wrong. As he reviews the disastrous dinner time he might say to himself, "What was I thinking to have got the preparation of a simple meal so wrong?" That is exactly the right question. What was I thinking?

Being able to address and answer that question is an example of metacognitive thinking and is a first step toward serving up a great meal. The key to solving the problem of a badly timed meal is an understanding that one of the thinking tools being used was sequencing and this is the part of the task that went wrong. The novice cook is helped greatly in this dinner time problem-solving if he is able to recognize the problem lay with his *sequencing* and then examine how his sequencing went wrong and determine how to fix it.

When we think clearly about our own thinking, we develop the ability to monitor and adjust our thinking when we don't seem to be getting anywhere. We understand that there are many different thinking tools that we can utilize to solve problems and we know how to select the most appropriate. Of course, we need the words to think about our thinking. Most of our complex thought processes are entirely dependent on our ability to find the right words.

TAKING THE TIME AND HAVING THE RIGHT WORDS

We hear a great deal about attention deficit as a way of explaining why so many of our children have difficulty focusing on one task and persisting until something is completed. While we are not qualified to make pronouncements about something that is in fact a medical diagnosis, we would suggest that in day-to-day life we could look at "attention deficit" in a different way. The problem may not be simply that our children cannot pay attention, rather they pay too much attention to too many things, more or less at the same time. They are not attention deficient, but they are attention overloaded. Their attention is being constantly directed to one new and interesting thing after another.

It isn't just children. As we transition from reading "dead tree" newspapers to online news sources, many people find themselves reading articles from beginning to end less frequently than they used to. Gone are the days when you would sit down at the breakfast table, in your train seat, or in an easy chair and open up the paper. Some people would flick through the paper looking for a particular section and then carefully fold the paper so that they could hold the broadsheet comfortably and then read the entire article.

Turning from page to page, article to article, was a physical task as well as a reading task. The newspaper needed to be repeatedly opened and folded and refolded. We committed considerable energy to each item we chose to focus on in our reading and so we tended to give it the extended attention of reading the entire article. The electronic newspaper requires no such physical manipulation. We can skim from headline to headline, section to section with a flick of a finger or a mouse. It is just so easy to skim.

It is also very easy to become distracted by the temptations of hyperlinks. In an article on coal seam gas we might see a blue word underlined, a hyperlink, and we know that clicking on that will take us to a different source of information and it just might be more interesting, or might add an extra dimension to the original article we were reading. So we click it, and pretty soon we come across another underlined blue word that looks promising, and so we click that.

Martin tried this recently. He began reading an article titled "Can business save us from climate change?" (*The Conversation*, April 16, 2014, http://theconversation.com/can-business-save-us-from-climate-change-25447). Within the first couple of paragraphs he was tempted by a link to an article in the *New York Times* (http://www.nytimes.com/2014/01/24/science/earth/threat-to-bottom-line-spurs-action-on-climate.html?_r=1), so he clicked on it and within that article he found a link to a report by the World Bank (http://www.worldbank.org/en/news/feature/2014/01/23/davos-world-bank-president-carbon-pricing). He clicked that and while he was scanning this article he saw a link on the side of the screen via a headline "Prosperity for All: Ending Extreme Poverty." Of course, that sounded fascinating so off he went.

Do you see what we mean? As he skittered across the surface of this set of issues he thought about nothing in depth. So it is sometimes with our children. It is not that they don't pay attention, they simply pay attention to too many things because there are so many things available to them. It's so much fun to play in the shallows. We need to give our children the tools they need to leave the shallows and move with confidence into the deep end.

One of the first things we need to help our children do is to disconnect from their fascination with surfaces. The ability to disengage from the network (not necessarily the computer) for a while and think in depth about a defined subject or idea is powerful. We need to help them to select a single focus and then dig deeper. We need to help them to read one article through to the end, pursue one line of thought until they feel they understand it. We need to help them develop the linear features of their brains rather than discard them in favor of the networked thinking that the electronic, digital age encourages so actively.

Yes, our children are thinking differently and the world is starting to look like a very different place. We explored the changing face of society in chapter 3 and explained subsequently why it is so important that we recognize these changes, accept the speed of change, and learn to inhabit this dynamic world *with* our children. But we have spent thousands of years becoming a sophisticated literate society. Our ancestors understood the value of linear, logical thought and thinking in depth. Every successful new development in society finds ways to embed the valuable qualities of the past. These values may be massaged and adjusted, but we will never get very far if we simply throw out the old when we find something new. The new grows out of the old and a wise society sees how to preserve what was worthwhile from the past.

And so, while we work to help our children navigate the exciting terrain of this new electronic interconnected landscape, we must also teach them to stop and examine in detail the significant places they encounter, to follow through a single line of thought.

One of the most significant things they need to understand in depth is their own thinking. Once they have understood and mastered their own thinking processes they will have the capacity to become independent learners with the resources to understand and resolve problems they have never encountered before. They will know which thinking tools to bring to bear, and how to monitor the success of their thinking and they will be able to adjust their thinking strategies when things don't seem to be working out as well as they might.

We have already stated that in order to become metacognitive thinkers, our children must first disengage periodically from the excitement of the surface and take the time to dive deeper. But they need more than periods of disentanglement from network. They will also need to develop a particular vocabulary associated with the acts of thinking. We mentioned at the start of this chapter that if we want to talk about thinking we need to have these words available to us, and if we want our children to become good thinkers, they will need to have the words to talk about their thinking too.

Children learn vocabulary from infancy by hearing new words said in contexts that support their meaning. A baby learns the words "ball," "throw," "me," and "you" while playing a game with a parent that involves rolling a ball back and forth across the floor of the living room. Teaching thinking words is no different.

What are these thinking words? They are words like predict, compare, contrast, sort, classify, reflect, analyze, clarify, evidence, fact, opinion, prove, evaluate, explain, and conclusion. There are many more. If we make these a part of our conversation when talking with our children they will become a part of their vocabulary too and then they will be able to think and talk about their own thinking because they will have the words to do it, they will move beyond the superficial response "because" when asked why they have a particular opinion or why they acted in a particular fashion.

Don't imagine that your children are going to find these words too difficult to understand. As long as they are presented in context, in the real world, children can incorporate a considerable number of apparently difficult words into their vocabularies, even if they sometimes find their own idiosyncratic pronunciations. Just listen to any small boy talk about dinosaurs.

Helping our children with this doesn't require anything special of us other than a shift in focus. As adults we need to develop a new habit. In quiet, unobtrusive ways we need to shift how we talk with young people. We need to find more opportunities to ask our children rather than tell our children. For some of us this can be quite a challenge.

↝ If your child is helping to fold and put away the clean laundry, instead of telling them where to put their socks and shorts, ask them where they think would be a good place. If they suggest somewhere different from where they are currently stored, ask the strategic question, "Oh? Why would you put them there instead of where they are kept now?" If we want our children to think it pays to think, give them the time to do it. This may mean a pause in the proceedings. Putting away the laundry may take a little longer. If the new place for the socks is based on good thinking then clearly the socks need to be moved. The child needs to see that thinking actually affects what happens in the world.

We have already mentioned that children sometimes have a favorite response when asked questions like this and you have probably heard it—"Because." But that isn't a reason, it's an evasion, and another gently probing question needs to follow—"What do you mean by 'because'?" Here is where we need to tread lightly, because there is an important line between questioning and interrogating that we do not want to cross. Children do not think well when they feel under threat.

THINKING AT SCHOOL AND AT HOME

Metacognitive thinking can be woven into most activities at school and into the simplest daily tasks at home. Asking students how they came to a conclusion, to describe the steps in solving a problem, and to interrogate the effectiveness of one problem-solving strategy over another all encourage metacognitive thinking. At home, in addition to questions about putting away the laundry you might ask your children to think of a better way to store kitchen dishes and utensils so that emptying the dish washer is a simpler and more straightforward task.

The key is to encourage them to think about why they make the decisions they do, to think about their first thoughts, to predict what the consequences might be, for example, of putting all the pots and pans in a very high cupboard and the sharp cooking knives in with the table cutlery. "Why would you do it that way and not some other way?" is a powerful metacognitive question.

Not everything needs to be dealt with in this way. The classroom is a busy place and sometimes we need to move through tasks briskly. Dealing with discipline issues can offer opportunities for metacognitive thinking, but if tempers are running hot and fists are flying, some more immediate action is needed. Pat recalls the time she was confronted by a situation in the playground where a twelve-year-old boy was swinging a baseball bat wildly to keep other children at bay. He was out of control and the situation needed cooling down immediately. Once the other children in the area had been removed and the lad had calmed down, they were able to walk and talk for a while. Gradually the opportunity arose to examine his feelings and his thoughts at the time, and over the coming days an effort was made to get him to think about his own thinking and what had led him into feelings of overpowering rage.

Parents are often very busy people and sometimes the situation demands a quick response rather than a more protracted thinking process. High emotions, for example, must be brought down to manageable levels before we can expect children to think in depth. We need to allay the fight or flight reactions and look for opportunities to help our children learn how to think well that are free from anger, anxiety, or a need for rebellion.

Asking a screaming four-year-old to think about how the other child might be feeling or to predict the consequences of belting his brother over the head with a toy bat won't get us very far. Later, when things have calmed down might be the time to talk through the problem and encourage the four-year-old to examine and so to recognize how and what he was thinking when he was so upset.

It helps, too, if our children believe that we value their thinking. The child learning to ride a bicycle usually receives a lot of praise and encouragement from parents as the wobbles become less frequent and she takes off in a straight line, balanced and in control. We offer up cries of delight and applause when our children take their first steps. How do we celebrate the steps our children take in the development of their most powerful skill, the ability to think well?

Attitude is very important. When a child expresses an opinion with which you disagree you can say something like, "How on earth did you come to that conclusion?" That sort of response almost guarantees the end of the conversation because the child feels challenged and devalued. It's a bit like telling him how clumsy he is when he falls off his bike in the early stages of learning to ride. It suggests you have little faith in his ability to think (or ride) and will more likely lead to him giving up rather than having another shot.

A much more encouraging response might have been "That's interesting. I would not have come to that conclusion. How did you get there? Is there another way we could think about it?" In other words, you are encouraging your child to get back up and try again, but this time with some coaching from you and with some consideration of technique and how to improve it.

Some of our youngest children are able to be metacognitive thinkers. We visited a small rural school where children from years 1, 2, and 3 were all in the same room. Working with the children we did some mental arithmetic. At the conclusion of the activity Pat asked the children how they had gone about working out their answers. One child said he had kept a picture in his head of the counters that were being used, another that she used a number line, and a third child stated that he remembered his number facts and used those to get to the answers. The value of exploring the "how" of the activity rather than only considering the outcome was that every child in that classroom learned that there were at least three different ways to solve the same problem.

We know that it is far more valuable for a child to learn multiple different ways to solve one problem than to solve multiple problems in one way. We want flexible thinkers, people who can see the same issue from a variety of viewpoints. If we focus only on the solutions to problems we miss out on the opportunity to be flexible. Metacognitive thinking—talking about how you solved it—is of enormous value.

The Common Core State Standards (CCSS) in its introduction to Mathematics describes one of the Key Shifts in thinking about mathematics teaching:

> Rather than racing to cover many topics in a mile-wide, inch-deep curriculum, the standards ask math teachers to significantly narrow and deepen the way time and energy are spent in the classroom.

One of the most effective and valuable ways to *deepen* understanding is to think metacognitively, and to investigate how we get to a solution rather than simply focus on whether or not the solution is correct.

It goes on to say that:

> Students must be able to access concepts from a number of perspectives in order to see math as more than a set of mnemonics or discrete procedures.

At every level of mathematics in the CCSS the Introduction states that students are expected to:

> Make sense of problems and persevere in solving them.
> Reason abstractly and quantitatively.
> Construct viable arguments and critique the reasoning of others.

It is only by identifying one's own reasoning and the reasoning of others that a student can critique that reasoning.

Consider this grade 5 CCSS mathematics standard:

> Relate volume to the operations of multiplication and addition and solve real world and mathematical problems involving volume. (CCSS.MATH.CONTENT.5.MD.C.5)

Whenever we ask students to solve real-world problems we give them an opportunity to explore possible strategies. The key for metacognitive thinking is not simply to discover the volume of a particular object, but to also explore the kinds of thinking that would enable a person to discover the volume.

After posing the problem of finding out the volume of a box with given linear measurements, teacher A might ask the students to work out the volume and give their answer. The teacher's response would only relate to the correct answer.

~~ Teacher B, on the other hand, is not always interested in the solu.. She wants her students to be accurate but she also wants to know about the process they used, understanding that:

- Students should be encouraged to find alternative ways of solving problems.
- While each student may only pursue one line of reasoning, by listening to the solutions of others they may discover different approaches.
- Sometimes the process may be appropriate, interesting, or perhaps even novel, but there is an error in calculation.
- By focusing on the process students are able to critique their own reasoning.

In the Introduction to the English Language Arts Standards of the CCSS, one of the key design considerations is expressed this way:

> ... *the Standards do not mandate such things as a particular writing process or the full range of metacognitive strategies that students may need to monitor and direct their thinking and learning. Teachers are thus free to provide students with whatever tools and knowledge their professional judgment and experience identify as most helpful for meeting the goals set out in the Standards.*

Since the fundamental purpose of the CCSS is to ensure students are college, career, and life ready, then there is no reason why we cannot use real-life examples in order to further the development of their metacognitive thinking strategies. We know that we are more likely to engage with adolescent students when we address the issues that have relevance to them.

Some examples of adults encouraging metacognition are as follows.

EXAMPLE A

~~ Let's consider a very different complex imaginary but real-world example and how it could be used to demonstrate the value of metacognitive thinking. A sixteen-year-old girl comes into class and announces that she has been invited to a party at a friend's home and she wants to attend but her parents will not let her. She is clearly upset and in no mood for the lesson you had prepared.

You understand that the decision is for the parent to make but you also see this as an engaging opportunity for this student and the others in the class to understand and extend their own thinking. Sometimes parties are not always well supervised and there is the risk that there may be alcohol. What do you do? You can choose to wash your hands of the problem and tell her it is none of your business, and it's entirely up to her parents. Another option is to use this as an opportunity to practice some thinking and some metacognition while addressing the issue in a way that ensures you are not interfering with the decisions that parents have the right to make.

The goal will be to get these students thinking, without making them feel defensive or that they are being interrogated. That's not always easy, and can be even more difficult when dealing with hypersensitive adolescents who seem to shed a protective layer of skin during their teenage years. Perhaps a good beginning would be to ask them to tell you what they know about these partiers and why they like to attend them. One of the first steps in good thinking is to amass some data or information.

There are three fairly straightforward steps to questioning that help avoid that feeling of interrogation youngsters resist so hard and to encourage something more than a glib, off the cuff response.

Setting the stage for any fruitful exchange is important and so it is essential that you actively listen. Stop what you are doing, make friendly eye contact, and focus on what the other person is actually saying. The trick here is to avoid, at all costs, the temptation to begin rehearsing what you intend to say next. Just listen.

Once the request for information has been made it is time to:

Pause
Paraphrase
Probe

Thoughtful conversations that encourage youngsters to think metacognitively are a kind of interweaving dance that uses these three strategies of pausing, paraphrasing, and probing. Each is brought in as it is needed and as it contributes to deepening the level of thinking.

Pausing is powerful. You need to provide enough time for the young person to respond and then, noticing that you are still waiting in anticipation of something more, perhaps add something to that initial response. We have all been in the position where we ask how the day has been and simply received the reply, "Fine." Where do you go from there? You pause, looking clearly as if you are expecting more. Maintain the relaxed eye contact, don't look challenging, and simply ... pause.

Paraphrasing involves repeating what the other person has said in your own words. This serves two very important purposes. When you paraphrase what the other person has said you make it clear to them that you have been listening, that your mind was on the conversation. It also offers the opportunity for the other person to correct or clarify anything that you might have either misheard or misinterpreted in what they said. It might go something like this:

> *Student:* Everyone's going to a party on Saturday night. I would like to go. They've got a pool so we can swim too.
> *Teacher:* So all your friends are going and you'd really like to go because there will be swimming, right?

Note that the teacher has not yet given any opinion about who should or should not attend the party. This is very deliberate, because the goal here is to get the students to think and then to think more deeply. Giving an opinion too soon will simply shut the conversation down. We want students to be able to think about the validity of their first thoughts, to think metacognitively—to think about their own thinking.

We want some more thinking but we also want some more information, more data, so this is the time for some *probing* question or two as well as a paraphrase of the students' responses.

> *Teacher:* What are some of the things your parents might want to know about any party you want to attend?
> *Student:* They probably want to know who will be there and if it will be supervised.
> *Mother:* So parents like to know there will be responsible adults at parties.
> *Student:* Yep.

Step 3 involves asking another question, a question that will *probe* a little more deeply and require the students to think more precisely.

> *Teacher:* How do you think a parent might find out a bit more about how these parties have been organized and supervised in the past? I think we need some more *information* so that we can make an *informed* decision, don't you?

Let's assume that the students are able to provide more information. What next? Some judicious questioning about the sources and the reliability of the information might be in order. Note that this is all entirely about obtaining data, not about giving opinions.

You might want to ask the students to group the information they have about the party under two headings—what you know to be the case and what you think is the case. We are asking students to think about the evidence on which we base decisions and to evaluate that evidence. This skill may be being developed in the context of a party, but it can be transferable to other more directly curriculum-related areas.

Predicting on the basis of given information is one of the thinking tools we mentioned earlier

Teacher: I have heard from parents that they are worried because sometimes kids smuggle alcohol into parties. If that happened can you *predict* what might happen next?
Student: That's not going to happen at this party.
Mother: OK. So what *evidence* are you using to feel confident that this couldn't happen?

Once this issue has been teased out, the discussion might move to predicting what the consequences might be if alcohol did find its way into the party, concluding with something like this:

Teacher: OK. Now we have this information. We have made some predictions of possible problems and we have created some reasonable plans to deal with our predictions. Do you think it is safe for me to say you can go to the party?

These students are being asked to think deeply about an issue and then to evaluate the quality of their thinking. Hopefully they have learned something about the importance of reliable information before making decisions. Having collected information they have then had the opportunity to make predictions that are valid because they are made on the basis of that evidence.

The teacher is helping these students to understand that decisions are best made when we feel sure that we have thought effectively. This process takes time, patience, and effort. It would have been so much easier to express an opinion at the start and move on, but to have done so would not have helped prepare the students to gradually take over their own decision making within the curriculum as well as in life.

The teacher is giving students some of the tools they need to become confident decision makers and problem-solvers, adults who can think about their own thinking and adjust it so that they feel confident about the validity of the decisions they make.

EXAMPLE B

A lad comes home or back into the classroom after lunch very upset about an altercation he has had with one of his classmates. Words were said, by him, by his classmate, and by others who were in the vicinity. He has taken all that in. In addition, there had earlier been several tweets back and forth and a few postings on his Facebook page. He has already developed a general understanding of what happened and what it means for him from all of these interconnected sources of information. Now is the time for him to disentangle from that. He doesn't need to ignore it, but he does need to begin a different kind of thinking and adults can help by the way they talk with him.

By getting him to think about his own reactions to the information he has taken in from all these sources, he is able to understand better what he is thinking, to evaluate whether his thinking is appropriate and helpful and, if necessary, he can work to change his thinking.

He will use lots of different thinking tools as he unravels what is going on, and you can help him if you use the language of thinking so that he will learn how to identify them himself in future. Knowing the name of a tool is always helpful when faced with a future decision about what tool to use.

As you talk with him you will hopefully nudge him toward useful thinking tools with questions and suggestions such as these:

Let's analyze the kinds of things people said about what they saw. Were they mostly positive or negative?

If you try and *remember* the interactions you have had with these people in the past, who do you *judge* have been the wisest and most loyal to their friends?

Whose opinions do you *value* most highly? Is there something about those people that make them more worth listening to? What is the *evidence* for that?

Can you *sort* through some of the comments people have made and just eliminate the ones that came from people whose opinions you don't value? Why do you discount some?

Putting yourself in Joe's shoes for a moment, what might he feel about your remarks?

What *alternatives* do you have?

Can you *predict* what might be the consequences if you do that? If you compare them, do some consequences matter more than some others?

Can you *plan* a course of action for when you get to school tomorrow? Let's take it one step at a time.

These are just suggestions, but each of these questions is designed not to interrogate but to encourage thinking, and each time a decision is made, the question, either implied or asked out loud, needs to be "why that and not something else?". This kind of discussion is helping your child to draw his own road map, to develop the skills needed to navigate his way through the future. Sometimes these sorts of discussions can be lengthy and at other times they might be brief and in passing. That's all in the timing.

TIMING

Timing can be critical. Imagine this real-life scene. One of a pair of three-year-old siblings is having a tantrum. She is livid, furious, and out of control. The source of her anger may or may not be her sister, and it's hard to know. As she rockets around the living room she grabs at each of her sister's playgroup paintings that are lovingly blue tacked to the walls. She pulls each one off the walls and rips it up, then drops it to the floor and stomps on it before moving on to the next one. She is crying copiously.

Her father, a great believer in thinking things through, is walking behind her asking her "What is making you so upset Penny?" "What do you thinking Susan is going to feel when she sees what you've done to her paintings?" and "How would you feel if Susan did this to your paintings?" Meanwhile little Penny continues with her mayhem and destruction. What was needed in this situation was action, not words. Penny was in no mood for talk, let alone thought.

And so, if your daughter comes home after the altercation at school with a red face and running nose, if she storms into the house, slamming the front door, throws her school bag across the kitchen floor and rushes upstairs to her room, this is probably not the time to follow her and ask her to analyze the things people have been saying about her online. Just as it is very difficult to think deeply when we are threatened, it is also difficult when we are in the thrall of strong emotions.

THE POWER OF QUESTIONS

🖋 Let's look a little more closely at questions. They are great starters for thinking but when used skillfully they are remarkably powerful in helping our children to get from the shallow end of thinking to the deep end.

Some questions are straightforward and simply elicit a direct response. They do not lead to further reflection. If the question "What is seven times eight?" is answered correctly that is probably the end of the discussion. If, however, it is followed with "How do you know that is correct?" we are encouraging a level of thinking far deeper than just recalling a fact or the final product of a series of thoughts.

Questions that begin with "what, when, where and who" often refer simply to remembered information or to the *products* of previously completed thinking, the end results. If you ask a child "What will you investigate for your next school project?" you are asking about the end point of his think. Questions such as "What will you do about the online bullying problem you are facing?" "Who is your best friend?" "When will you be home?" "Where are you going this afternoon?" or "What is your favorite movie?" all focus on the end products of thinking. That's not necessarily a superficial or minimal thing.

We need those kinds of answers. But we are trying to help our youngsters develop the kinds of thinking that will help guarantee those answers are all good answers, well considered, based on a foundation of skilled thinking.

Some of these kinds of questions can be quite complex. To answer them we may need to do quite a bit of sorting and sifting through all the things we believe we know about the subject.

Consider this question: "What are some of the most important issues in the upcoming election?" This is a "wh" question and in order to answer it adequately one needs to know quite a bit about all of the issues facing the government and then make some evaluative judgments about their relative significance. Furthermore, it is open-ended—you are not asking about one issue but several, and this prompts an organization of the issues into a sequence. This is a different order of thinking from that required to answer a question like this: "What is the fourth letter of the alphabet?"

If you have a good answer to some of these sorts of questions, it means that you have probably already done quite a bit of thinking. Of course, it is also possible that the answer has been arrived at almost spur of the moment, with very little thought. We really can't learn much at all about the effectiveness of the thinking that went on if we focus only on the product of the thinking.

It is also possible that the answers were simply the thoughtless regurgitation of things that have been found online. The Internet is awash with opinion as well as information.

HOW AND WHY

⇝ "Wh" questions can tax our ability to think, but "how" and "why" questions cause us to think at a different level—they can be metacognitive questions. Asking "how" and "why" cause us to examine our own thinking processes, and to evaluate the extent to which we are thinking effectively. These sorts of questions focus on the *process* of thinking rather than the product. It is only when we are sure the process was adequate that we can feel confident in the product. Only when we know why and how we came to the conclusion we did, can we know it was a valid conclusion.

When we understand the processes of our thinking, we can also know about the success or otherwise of our thinking. We are then in a position to modify or adjust how we are thinking to ensure that is effective and efficient for the tasks at hand. Asking "how" and "why" can be very powerful because they encourage metacognitive thinking, and they cause us to examine our own thinking.

If you ask a child "What will you buy with your allowance this week?" you will get a list, long or short, but if you ask, "How will you decide what to buy with your allowance?" the thinking process enters the deep end and the child begins to think metacognitively—to become aware of, and think about his own thinking.

There are many different ways to word the prompts that can lead to metacognitive thinking—thinking about our thinking. The question "How did you work out the answer to that problem?" puts the child into this deep end thinking. We could rephrase that question as a "wh" question by asking "What steps did you take in solving that problem?" "Wh" questions can elicit metacognitive thinking. It all depends on how they are used and whether they are used with the intention of getting to the process rather than the product.

REMEMBERING AND UNDERSTANDING

If we want our children, and indeed, ourselves, to think metacognitively, then an understanding of what is involved in this thing called "thinking" is pretty important. There are many different kinds of thinking and we engage in most of them every day. We remember things such as the date, the names of our children, and the things we need to buy at the supermarket. We also remember quite complex things such as how to drive home from to work, how to perform a particular stroke in golf, how to fit a new washer to a leaky tap, and, perhaps, the long history of political debate leading up to the present moment. Some things we remember are facts, some are behavioral routines and others are complex sequences of physical actions and some are complex memories of past events or thoughts.

BLOOM'S TAXONOMY AND METACOGNITION

We briefly mentioned Benjamin Bloom and his taxonomy of learning in chapter 1. Let's explore some of his ideas in a little more detail. Sometimes we can remember things without necessarily understanding them. We might remember that the First World War is said to have been started by the assassination of Arch Duke Ferdinand, but that doesn't mean we understand anything much about that statement—who was Arch Duke Ferdinand, why would his death have meant so much, was it something about him or about the man who shot him, and why was he shot? We might recall that in order to divide one fraction by another we should turn the second fraction upside down and then multiply them. That doesn't mean we understand the process. So understanding is a different kind of thinking.

APPLYING

Understanding can lead to yet another valuable kind of thinking—the application of what is understood to the resolving of some issue, the solving of a problem or the deeper understanding of something else. I may remember the routine for dividing fractions (even if I don't quite understand it) but can I apply this to a real-life situation? If I really don't understand what I am doing when I carry out this routine, how can I effectively apply it? If, however, I understand the dictionary meaning of a word, then I can use it sensibly in a well-formed sentence. If I understand the rules of accounting I can apply them and manage the books of a small company. By understanding things I am able to do important things in the real world.

ANALYZING

The ability to analyze things is another kind of thinking. When we analyze something we seek to identify its parts and come to an understanding about how they relate to one another. We look to find the ways in which things are organized. Through analysis we understand the interrelationships within systems.

A weather forecaster analyzes all the data he is receiving about air pressure, sea currents, humidity, wind speeds and direction, and more, and as a result of that analysis he is able to come to an understanding of the weather systems that are currently affecting us and what might be in store for us tomorrow. His ability to understand rests on the foundations of two other kinds of thinking we have already described. He needs to have remembered what he has learned about each of the various elements he is analyzing and he needs to understand how they each behave and interact with one another. The more complex our thinking becomes, the more it tends to rely on various other kinds of thinking.

SYNTHESIZING

When we think we also frequently put things together, we synthesize information and thoughts. Much of our understanding of other people and our development of strong relationships is a result of the synthesis over time of all we know and come to know about other people. A couple meets at a friend's house for the first time. They are attracted to one another physically and during the evening they talk about a wide-ranging set of topics. At the end of the night they have gathered a certain amount of information about each other and are beginning to develop a sense of one another that suggests they would like to get to know more. They arrange to meet again. As time goes by, this couple spends a considerable amount of time together and at each meeting they learn something new.

Over time an understanding grows about who the other person is, and what their values, interests, and priorities are. Each new piece of information is synthesized with what has already been learned until they feel they understand one another. They may make the decision that their lives are so compatible that they may commit to a domestic partnership, they may decide to remain good friends, or they may come to the conclusion that they are so different and perhaps at odds with one another that it would be best to limit any further interactions. We come to understand people and situations by synthesizing all the various pieces of information we accumulate.

We can also find ourselves needing to synthesize two or more complex systems. We would hope that our teenage children are developing a system of ethics that will give them a foundation for decisions about the rightness and wrongness of their behavior in the future. We also want them to understand and internalize a desire for achievement. Sometimes these two complex areas can come into seeming conflict.

A young man has worked very hard in mathematics at school. He knows he must get a very good grade in his final exams in order to move on to university. He has no doubt that he has put in the effort required and he understands the relationship between effort and result. He is half way through his paper when he is faced with a problem that requires him to recall a particular formula and that formula has gone completely out of his head.

He knew it yesterday but he just cannot recall now when he needs it most. He glances across to his left and can just see the paper that his neighbor is working on. He realizes he is up to the same question. Should he try and surreptitiously locate the formula on his neighbour's paper? He knows he will recognize it the moment he sees it. Or is this cheating? This young man is facing a common situation—he needs to synthesize his moral beliefs with his desire for success.

EVALUATING

When we are planning to purchase a new home we are faced with many opportunities for synthesizing our thoughts. We have a set of wants and needs in a house, but we also have a set amount of money. Whenever we are required to synthesize information we may find ourselves also required to evaluate. Evaluating is another form of thinking. When we evaluate we set one thing against another and make judgments about their relative merits or value. Is it acceptable to cheat when you know that you really understand the work but have just had a momentary lapse of memory? If we buy this house will it justify the additional expense and the consequence that the family will have to forego an annual holiday for a few years to come?

CREATING

Perhaps one of the most interesting kinds of thinking is creative thinking. Professor Kenneth Robinson defines creative thinking as "The process of having original ideas that have value" (TED video). Every significant step forward that has occurred in the world has been the result of someone having a new idea that was valuable. Many people have expressed their concern that our present education systems, with their focus on teaching things that can be readily tested, are neglecting this most important kind of thinking—creative thinking. Creative thinking is often unpredictable and so it is very difficult, and sometimes impossible, to develop a test that measures the capacity for creative thinking since the end product cannot be determined ahead of time.

Educators know that these kinds of thinking—remembering, understanding, analyzing, synthesizing, and creating—are a few examples of the thinking skills we find in Bloom's Taxonomy. We looked briefly at the influence of Benjamin Bloom in chapter 1. He was an American educational psychologist who sought to further develop our understanding of learning by analyzing it and developing a structure that would describe it. He identified three distinct domains of learning, the affective domain, the psychomotor domain, and the cognitive domain.

The affective domain of learning analyzes how people learn emotionally, and how they become able to empathise with others, see another's point of view, and develop an awareness of the emotional needs of a society.

He also wrote about the psychomotor domain. Here he categorized the physical skills that we need to survive and to prosper in our society. These include such survival skills as perception and reaction, as well as the learned skills of walking and talking and encompassing the skills needed to carry out complex tasks such as writing, painting, playing a musical instrument, using a scalpel, or playing sports.

Bloom's third domain was cognition and it was here that he classified thinking into these separate categories: remembering, understanding, applying, analyzing, synthesizing, and evaluating. Other theorists, such as Anderson and Krathwohl, have revised Bloom's list and added the category of creative thinking.

When we talk about thinking about our thinking, or metacognition, one of the first things we need to be able to do is to identify the kind of thinking we are doing. When we are faced with a problem to solve, we need to know what kinds of thinking to bring to bear and we need to know how to use each kind of thinking both appropriately and effectively. Thinking is a tool. If you want to cut a piece of stainless steel you need to select the right kind of saw and the right kind of saw blade. You need to know how to use the implement. So it is with thinking.

In a world where we are swimming in an almost bottomless sea of information, where new information becomes available at the click of a hyperlink, and where rapid change is inevitable, the most fundamental skill we must teach our children and young people is how to think. Some observers of society have pointed to dangerous consequences if we fail to this successfully. In his book *What the Internet Is Doing to Our Brains: The Shallows* Nicholas Carr warns (Carr, 2010) us:

> The great danger we face as we become more intimately involved with our computers—as we come to experience more and more of our lives through the disembodied symbols flickering across our screens—is that we we'll begin to lose our humanness, to sacrifice the very qualities that separate us from machines. The only way to avoid that fate ... is to have the self awareness and the courage to refuse to delegate to computers the most human of our mental activities and intellectual pursuits.

GIST THINKING

The kind of self-awareness this book is discussing is the kind that comes with metacognitive thinking. Carr is particularly concerned about the influence that the Internet can have on attention. He argues that the sheer volume of stimulation and of competing messages that we are subjected to whenever we go online trains our brains to be distracted. Distraction becomes the norm.

A colleague, who is a university professor, was recently bemoaning what she saw as a growing tendency toward what she called "gist thinking" among her students. Their tendency to skim information, to be readily distracted from one Google search to the next, until they had pieced together a kaleidoscope of bits and pieces into an overall sense of something, was very worrying to her.

In a study published in 2010 it was found that "students ... have non-course related software applications open and active about 42% of the time" during undergraduate lectures. And this was in the days before the pervasive influence of text messaging and other social media became as firmly entrenched in our waking hours as they are now (Kraushaar and Novak, 2010).

Carr talks about people becoming "chronic scatterbrains." For many people researching a subject involves jumping from link to link on the Internet. A question or topic is typed into the search engine and a list of possibilities opens up. We select one and read the bit that interests us, before jumping to the next and the next and the next. All of these bits and pieces gradually form a kind of networked web of understanding that, while superficial in some ways, may also be very valuable. This is "gist thinking" but it isn't necessarily bad. This kind of networked thinking is very different from the linear, intensive thinking of the literate, industrial, predigital world.

We need to teach our kids how to navigate the rich, interconnected world of the Internet. We need to encourage them to make connections, to link old knowledge with new discoveries, to create networks in their understandings that are essentially horizontal, broad, and integrating. But we also need to make sure they see the value of deep thinking, of mining at depth a rich seam of knowledge. There is a place for "gist" thinking, but it doesn't replace deep thinking. The digital generation will only become a generation of "chronic scatterbrains" if we allow ourselves to believe that the new has somehow replaced the old. It hasn't.

When television became a fixture in almost every living room in the developed world we heard predictions that the cinema was doomed. Why, people asked, would anyone want to go out in the cold and pay money to sit with strangers and watch a movie when they do the same thing in the comfort and familiarity of their own home? But it wasn't the same thing, and movie cinemas have become multiplexes and bigger and better movies are made each year. The experience is different, sitting in the complete dark, uninterrupted, with a huge wall-sized screen and surround sound. It's a social act, and it's a part of the pleasures most take in going out for the evening. We still love to go to the movies.

Something similar was said of the CD and DVD. When they appeared on the market we began to look askance at our trusty tape recorders and wondered how long it would be before we gave into this new-fangled idea and bought a CD or DVD player. It didn't take long. You would be hard pressed to buy a tape or tape player today. The new medium has replaced the old. Why? Because it does the same thing, only better. Audiophiles may disagree, but for the average set of human ears and eyes there is no loss and, indeed, significant gain with high-definition DVDs. A new medium replaces an old, a new way of doing things replaces an old way, when the new way does the same things (and sometimes even more) and does them better.

The kind of linear, literate thinking we have learned through the ages is not the same as the networked, interactive "gist" thinking encouraged by the Internet. They serve different purposes. The danger is that the seductive qualities of these new ways of thinking will overwhelm the calmer, more considered and focused ways of thinking of the literate culture. That is why it is so important that we all ensure that our children, who are learning almost without our intervention, to be brilliant gist thinkers, also learn how to think in the deep end, to be metacognitive thinkers who understand how their brains and thinking processes work.

We can all play a part in this, those inside and outside the education world, within families and within communities. We are all a part of the "global village" that is raising our children, and we all have parts to play.

KEY IDEAS IN THIS CHAPTER

- We want young people to become independent learners, good team members, and cooperative and responsible citizens. We value these qualities over simply having knowledge of facts.
- The workforce is changing and flexibility and the ability to adapt is increasingly important.
- We must actively teach our children how to think.
- Most of our thinking is done almost unconsciously. Thinking in the deep end requires us to understand our thinking—to think about our thinking.
- Good thinkers can understand, monitor, evaluate, and regulate their thinking.
- There are many thinking tools we can use and we can teach our children to recognize them and know when to use them.
- The speed with which we can find digital information can encourage us to move rapidly through it without giving anything due attention or extended thought.
- It's important to disconnect and focus on just one thing if we are to become deeper thinkers.
- We also need to have the vocabulary to talk about our thinking.
- Children need to see that we value their thinking.
- Very young children can be metacognitive thinkers and metacognition deepens understanding.
- The Common Core expects that we teach our children to think about and understand their own thinking.
- Timing is important if we want our children to think about their thinking.
- Metacognitive thinking can be woven into most tasks by asking "why" and "how."
- Bloom's taxonomy describes increasingly complex kinds of thinking.
- We can do a great deal to help our young people become something more than "gist thinkers" or "chronic scatterbrains."

DISCUSSION

- How would you describe the balance between remembering things and thinking about things in your school or class?
- Give some examples of lessons where kids have really started to think about how they are learning and how they are thinking. What was the impetus that got them beyond remembering or cranking the recall handle?
- Is gist thinking a problem in your experience? Consider ways of encouraging deeper and longer involvement.

Chapter Thirteen

Behaving Like a Deep-Water Thinker

We have all met people of whom we would say, "She really shoots from the hip," and others about whom we might comment, "He always thinks before he acts." These characteristics become a part of the individual's personality, Action Man versus The Philosopher. We see different behaviours in each of them, and some behaviours support deep water thinking better than others. Some people are inclined to jump in fast with the first thought in their minds.

Others will wait, process, and then give a considered comment. These dispositions help form their personalities. While we may love the enthusiasm of the Action Men, and may become impatient with The Philosopher, both bring different dispositions to the business of thinking. How do we develop the disposition to act in ways that will support effective thinking?

DISPOSITIONS FOR SUCCESSFUL THINKING

The Common Core State Standards (CCSS) states that:

The standards focus on core concepts and procedures starting in the early grades

But there is more to being college and career ready than learning concepts and procedures. There is more to education than simply being "college and career ready." We need to ensure that our students become "life ready." Being life ready includes being college and career ready, but it goes further.

The philosopher Soren Kierkegaard said, "Life can only be understood backwards; but it must be lived forwards." As our young people move forward in their lives we also want them to be able to reflect on what are learning and experiencing in order to understand themselves and the world within which they live. Of great importance is the ability to reflect on the kinds of behaviors that nurture learning and the growth of thoughtful living.

We need to move our attention to the personal context within which everything that has gone before will succeed or fail. We will explore the kinds of behaviors that make deep water thinking possible. This kind of thinking is a process and every kind of process requires the right conditions to flourish. Without sunshine the process of photosynthesis cannot occur. Without adequate nutrition the processes of growth and development will be stunted. Without a set of mutually agreed ground rules the process of debate will founder. Similarly without the right conditions the processes of effective thinking cannot be fully realized.

WHAT KINDS OF BEHAVIORS AND DISPOSITIONS ENABLE EFFECTIVE, DEEP THINKING TO FLOURISH?

Arthur Costa and Bena Kallick interviewed a large selection of people deemed to be successful and they distilled from their research a set of sixteen behaviors that they believed underpinned these people's successes. Costa and Kallick argued that a successful person is a person who knows how to effectively solve problems to which the answer is not immediately available (Costa and Kallick, 2008).

When faced with a difficult problem the successful person does not simply turn to a search engine, type in a question, and then act of the answer. The successful person has a repertoire of behaviors that can be called upon so that she can solve the problem herself. This may involve using the Internet or collaborating with others. The crucial thing is, however, that she is solving the problem herself and not simply relying on someone else's canned solution she found on the Internet.

In other words, what you do when you don't know what to do is the measure of your success in life. These behaviors provide the context, the conditions, for effective deep water thinking, they are to thinking what oxygen, fuel, and ignition are to the process of combustion. If we want our young people to be able to think in depth, they need to know how to behave.

Costa and Kallick described these behaviors as the "Habits of Mind." They used the word "habit" very deliberately, because the goal is that each behavior should become second nature, employed almost automatically when the thinking requires it. Just as we hope to make the cleaning of teeth before bed a habit in our children, so too we should strive to make these Habits of Mind behaviors that are employed as a matter of course when the appropriate time comes. We don't expect a small child to know how to clean his teeth, we teach him. Even as adults we frequently find ourselves having to brush up on our technique after some hints from the dental hygienist. So it is with these habits of thinking, the Habits of Mind.

But there is more to these habits than technique, just as there is more to tooth hygiene than brushing vertically. There must be an inclination to bring out the habit when it is needed. You know how it is when you come home very late from a dinner with friends and it seems all too hard to do anything but get undressed and hop into bed? Then something niggles at you and you just can't get into bed without cleaning your teeth too. That's how these Habits of Mind become when we have been consciously exercising them for a time.

When we have truly made them into habitual behaviors we find we are inclined toward them when they are needed, we don't feel right if we don't employ them when faced with problems that need solving, when we need to do some deep water thinking.

WHAT ARE THESE SIXTEEN HABITS OF MIND?

1. Persisting
2. Managing our impulsivity
3. Listening with understanding and empathy
4. Thinking flexibly
5. Thinking about our thinking (thinking metacognitively)
6. Striving for accuracy
7. Questioning and posing problems
8. Applying past knowledge to new situations
9. Gathering data through all our senses
10. Responding with wonderment and awe
11. Creating, imagining, innovating
12. Taking responsible risks
13. Finding humor
14. Thinking interdependently
15. Remaining open to continuous learning

For our purposes we will explore persisting, managing impulsivity, communicating with clarity and precision, and thinking interdependently. All sixteen habits are important but these four are particularly relevant when we examine the role of thinking in the networked world of this electronic age.

PERSISTING

The ability to persist is complex. To stick at something until it is mastered requires us to have resilience and optimism. We must have the ability to rebound from failure and try again when working on a difficult task. It is important to have the self-belief that tells us that we can succeed if we put in sufficient effort. We also need to be able to find alternative ways to solve a problem if our first attempt isn't working. In other words, we need to be flexible thinkers—one of the other Habits of Mind. But it is absolutely paramount that we have the ability to focus clearly on what we are trying to achieve and to maintain that focus as we progress, sometimes agonizingly slowly, sometimes swiftly, toward that goal.

Our experiences shape our brains and the "neurons that fire together, wire together." It is a characteristic of both game playing and Internet surfing that attention is being constantly switched from one thing to another. Research suggests that we typically look for very short periods at any one page on the Internet and our own personal experiences demonstrate the seductive power of the hyperlink where we can drill down and around a topic by clicking on link after link. Games are incredibly fast paced and require large numbers of split second decisions at every point.

Youngsters can demonstrate considerable persistence when they are attempting to reach a higher level in a computer game. This is not the same kind of persistence that enables them to become thinkers in the deep end. That kind of thinking requires the sort of persistence that includes extended periods of focus and attention on a small number of things, not the scattered, fast paced attention of a game.

The fear of researchers is that this rapid switching of attention gets in the way of the brain developing the neuronal patterns needed for long-term memory and for persistence with a single, developing line of thought. Could it be that multitasking like this doesn't mean we become good at doing lots of things at the same time, rather that we never learn how to do any one thing effectively? Is the "gist thinking" we spoke of earlier a symptom of this developmental failure to focus and persist?

Of course, in such a new and expanding field of research there will be many differing views. It often takes a very long time for something to become settled in any new science and the deep understanding of how the brain works is very new indeed. The science is settled, however, on the fact that the brain is plastic and remains so throughout life.

Our experiences influence the physical "shape" of the brain by determining the nature of the neuronal paths and networks that develop. It is wise, therefore, to ensure that the experiences our youngsters encounter will promote the development of neural pathways that enable effective thinking and the capacities to focus and persist are fundamental. Once again we are talking about balance and arguing that we help our children and young people to develop both their linear, focused, literate brains AND their networked, dynamic, multitasking brains.

In examining the shifts in thinking about mathematics standards the CCSS state:

> The Common Core calls for greater focus in mathematics. Rather than racing to cover many topics in a mile-wide, inch-deep curriculum, the standards ask math teachers to significantly narrow and deepen the way time and energy are spent in the classroom.

In other words, the CCSS require that students have the tenacity to dig deeper in their understanding of mathematical concepts. Instead of leaping from one topic to the next, students are expected to persist in their examination of problems, to look for alternative solutions, discarding those that are unsatisfactory and seeking out those that work.

In grade 8 geometry, for instance, students are expected to:

> Know the formulas for the volumes of cones, cylinders, and spheres and use them to solve real-world and mathematical problems. (CCS, 2009. MATH. CONTENT.8.G.C.9)

It is clearly the intention of the CCSS that students be encouraged to look beyond the first, obvious solution to any problem, to think flexibly and creatively. Thinking more deeply is entirely dependent on having persistence.

Persistence requires focus. Dr Manfred Spitzer is a German neuroscientist and in his book "Digitale Demenz, 2012" he warns of the emergence and spread of something he calls "digital dementia." His work was preceded by observations made some years earlier in Korea by Dr Byun Gi-won of the Balance Brain Centre in Seoul.

Gi-won's argument was that the apparent addiction of Korean young people to electronic screens, gaming, the Internet, and their excessive interactions with digital media was leading to an undesirable rewiring of their plastic brains. He argued that the left side of the brain was the most heavily used during these Internet and gaming sessions and it was developing at the expense of the right hemisphere, which is more closely identified with concentration, memory, and attention. In order to persist we must concentrate, we must remember what we have done and we must pay focused attention.

We hear many adults complain that young people are intellectual butterflies nowadays, unable to concentrate on one thing for any length of time and lacking the capacity to focus to the completion of a task. This isn't a new criticism. The pervasive influence of commercial television was blamed twenty or even thirty years ago for the need for teaching content to be broken up into ten to twenty-minute chunks, with a commercial break in between. It was argued that watching television had conditioned our young people into being able to concentrate only for relatively short periods of time.

HOW DO WE ENCOURAGE THE DEVELOPMENT OF PERSISTENCE?

Provide an environment that allows for focus and persistent effort by minimizing or eliminating interruptions and distractions.

Encourage students to think before they leap into a problem. They will need to be sure they understand what the problem is asking of them, how to begin, what steps might be taken in the process of problem-solving, and what materials, information, or data will be needed. They need to make sure what they need will be available when they need it.

Sustained periods of silent reading give students the opportunity to settle into a book and become immersed.

Being able to put up with the silence after asking a question is a key to developing persistence in youngsters. Persistence is not encouraged when they know that you will move on, to another topic or another student, when there is no response immediately offered. Lengthen your wait time and see what happens.

Dividing complex tasks into smaller steps, and then tracking progress as each step is mastered, can help a student see that persisting gets results.

It isn't enough to tell a youngster to "stick at it" and "don't give up" when they are facing a difficult problem. We need to teach them a variety of ways to approach and solve a problem. It is much more valuable to know several different ways to solve one problem than it is to solve several problems in one way. Give children the opportunity to share with one another the methods they used to solve problems as we did with the mental arithmetic example in the previous chapter.

When engaged in online research, encourage your students to stop and evaluate rather than simply collect. If they are looking for information, for example, on the causes of the Great Depression, you can ask them to find two or three references that provide explanations and then to explain why they think those references are reliable. We want them to interact and make use of digital media, but we also require them to detach and focus, to evaluate and select carefully, and to think more deeply about what they find. "Does anyone think differently? Did anyone do it a different way?" These should be frequent questions, followed by "How do we know this is right or reasonable?"

MANAGING IMPULSIVITY

Effective thinking is also tied closely to our ability to manage our impulsive behaviors. By no means does this imply we should never be impulsive. Rather it means that we should know when it is advantageous to be impulsive and when we need to slow down and take a firmer control of our thinking behavior. In a sense this is what this entire book is all about—how to make the most of digital media and when to detach, slow down, and think deeply.

As discussed in the previous section, the rapid fire nature of the Internet and of gaming both mean that our youngsters have at their disposal a medium that actively promotes both multitasking and impulsivity. It is very easy to gain an impression of something, to garner a large field of initial responses or information about a topic.

There is great value in gist thinking when what you are seeking is the gist of something—the broad brush picture, without the details. The Internet is also a great place to get brainstorming ideas simply because of the speed with which we can flick from one source to another, one web page to another.

But managing impulsivity means knowing when to draw a halt to the rapid fire accumulation of ideas and information, when to sift through and identify what is really important or relevant and when to dig deeper and do some deep water thinking.

The networked, dynamic, interactive brain is valuable for some kinds of thinking and impulsivity puts to one side our judgmental faculties and gives our brains the freedom to think creatively, without the boundaries of convention. This is the very root of innovation and creative thinking—another of the Habits of Mind. The literate, logical, and linear brain is a powerful tool as well, and an effective thinker knows when to bring each one to the ascendancy.

To succeed in the world today our youngsters need to know when to be impulsive thinkers and when to be measured, controlled, and methodical thinkers. They need to know how and when to engage with the kaleidoscopic electronic world of information, and when to disentangle ourselves from it and think deeply. It's up to us to teach them.

ENCOURAGING THE MANAGEMENT OF IMPULSIVITY

On wet days, when kids are held inside the classroom during recess, it's worth providing them with some games and other activities to offset the tendency to riot!

Having thoughtful strategy games such as chess, draughts, connect four, Monopoly, Kensington, and scrabble all encourage slowing down, predicting, and thinking. New strategy games are being regularly added to the market.

Jigsaws are also a useful pastime for impulse management. There are a myriad of fast-paced, almost intuitive computer games that you could have available. In these you can only win if you don't stop to think. Make sure that you have a roster of games and ensure students cycle through different kinds of games. You then have a very rich platform of experience from which to launch a discussion about the differences between the games and the role of impulsivity. It's hard to manage something when you don't quite know what it is.

There is creativity in impulsivity. Give youngsters permission to be impulsive sometimes when brainstorming ideas. This is easier to do when you tell them that you value speed and number more than correctness on this occasion. Fill the board with ideas and suggestions and avoid value judgments at all cost.

Planning is one fairly sure fire way to avoid impulsive behaviors. It's not enough to set a project, ask "Does anyone have any questions?" and then leave them to get on with it. Who wants to be the first person to admit they don't know something when they suspect everyone else does? It is often not until you start trying to plan that you discover what you don't know. Spend some time exploring the nature of the task, describing the end point and plotting an action plan to get there. Don't labor it, but don't neglect it either.

We examined the power of questioning in the chapter on metacognition and this is another time when we can encourage the management of impulsivity. Make certain the young people with whom you deal understand that the first thing that comes into their heads isn't good enough. You can insist on a 30-second thinking time before anyone answers, or ask probing follow-up questions building on the first answer.

🖎 This small group activity encourages pausing for deeper thinking, with each student having the opportunity to both compose and answer questions. Students work in groups of three and number themselves. The teacher poses a question, writing it on the board. Student 1 proposes an answer to the question. Student 2 asks a question about that answer and student 3 offers an answer to the second question. This can be extended almost indefinitely.

> *Teacher's question:* What are the main impacts of drought?
> *Student 1's answer:* The lakes all dry up.
> *Student 2's question:* What happens if the lakes dry up?
> *Student 3's answer:* The people and animals that rely on the lake water will die.
> *Student 1's question:* Are lakes the only source of water for people and animals?
> *Student 2's answer:* No. There is water underground.
> *Student 3's question:* How could people and animals access water underground?
> *Student 1's answer:* By digging wells.... and so on.

Social behavior is fraught with problems arising out of failure to manage impulsivity, especially online social behavior. It is so easy to hit the "send" button. It takes no time at all for an Internet discussion to become a source of insult and hurt feelings. Help youngsters to understand the dangers of the "send" button.

We grown-ups need to encourage youngsters to stop, detach, and think before responding at times. Just as we teach children to walk away sometimes in the playground, we need to teach them the value of walking away from the device in order to have enough time to think.

Withholding judgment is hard enough for teachers. It can be equally difficult for young people who can be very critical of one another. Adolescent insecurity can lead to a view of the world that groups people into those like me and the rest. Life becomes a little easier when you are a part of a group, and so kids identify themselves, and others, as nerds, jocks, preppies, goths, emos, gamers, hipsters, and the list goes on. Making judgments comes easily. Withholding judgment requires tight management of impulsivity.

Helping young people to realize that they need to understand something before they judge is powerful learning. It also requires deep thinking. If you have youngsters who self-identify with any of these subcultures you can encourage some deep water thinking by providing safe opportunities for them to explain who they are and what they find attractive about their group.

Prejudice grows out of superficial, impulsive thinking and behavior.

COMMUNICATING WITH CLARITY AND PRECISION

The CCSS place particular emphasis on the student's ability to communicate with clarity and precision as demonstrated by these grade 11 and 12 Writing Standards:

> Write informative/explanatory texts to examine and convey complex ideas, concepts, and information clearly and accurately through the effective selection, organization, and analysis of content. (CCS, 2009, ELA-LITERACY.W.11–12.2)
> Use precise language, domain-specific vocabulary, and techniques such as metaphor, simile, and analogy to manage the complexity of the topic. (CCS, 2009, ELA-LITERACY.W.11–12.2.D)

As with all forms of language, the specifics of syntax and vocabulary are very context dependent. The 140-character limit of Twitter has led to the development of a new written language. How many of these commonly used twitter words do you recognize: b4, bfn, icymi, cu, lmao, rofl? Restricting an idea or a message to only 140 characters really pushes our ability to be precise and clear, wasting no words, getting right to the point. It has also been a medium for creativity with language as these new "words" so amply demonstrate.

Parents and teachers might fear that our children will forget how to spell words correctly when they use these extreme contractions, but the evidence shows a different picture. We all use different forms of our language in different circumstances. We expect our children to speak differently when talking with grandparents or with their mates in the playground. We write using different words and sentence structures when communicating with a business colleague about a business issue and the kind of letter or email we would write to a friend about arrangements for the Friday night football game.

Part of being a fluent user of any language involves understanding and being able to use its different forms appropriately. As long as we make it explicit that there is a different expectation when writing formal English, and as long as we teach our children what those expectations are, we need not fear that they will write out their job applications in Twitterese.

Social networking conversations are a different matter. When we engage face to face in a discussion we know that a huge amount of what is communicated is nonverbal. We communicate with our tone of voice, with the volume we use, with the expressions that cross our faces, and with the physical stance of our bodies. If someone takes a firm step toward you with their arms tightly folded across their chest and their voice raised, you will know something about the direction the discussion is taking. All these things are missing in an online discussion.

In an online discussion it might appear that all we have are the words. In fact we do sometimes have a little more than that. In some chat modes it is possible to see each key stroke as it is made. In those cases there can be subtle hints in the speed of the strokes, the pauses and hesitations, and the backtracking and rewording that we are able to watch taking place in real time. But on most social networking sites the thought is written down and then the enter key is hit.

The reader, or indeed the mass of readers, will only see the final form the writer has given to their thoughts. All we have are the words. Perhaps more importantly, the writer never sees the nonverbal reactions to the message. All the nonverbal cues that tell you that you have amused someone, made them angry, reminded them of something, hit a sensitive nerve or, indeed hurt their feelings, these are all absent.

Once again, the important thing is to move out of the shallows, escape from all that fascinating movement and light, slow down, and think a bit more deeply.

It can be fun to engage in these conversations but we need to keep our wits about us. We need to be on the lookout for the "trolls" and "flamers" whose only interest is to incite disagreement and strong feelings. We must help our children to learn how to choose their words carefully, how not to be trapped by the faulty thinking of others, and how to disengage from an online discussion when there is nothing worthwhile to be gained from continuing. We should help them in their attempts to manage their own impulsivity and learn to think carefully before hitting the enter button, to consider the potential consequences of the words they are about to send to readers they may not know as well as good friends.

There are safe forums where kids can learn the skills of online conversation. One is http://kidzworld.com/forums and another is http://community.scholastic.com/. These are primarily social forums with their own sets of rules and they state that they are closely moderated.

You could also set up a closed Facebook group with settings that only allow members of the class to interact. You can discuss and set up a list of rules for the group that might include the following:

- No discrimination, ridicule, or bullying.
- Stay on topic.
- Never post links to external web sites—you just don't know where they might lead.
- Read what a person has said before responding.
- Don't give out personal information.
- Don't talk about other people.
- Remember that all caps is SHOUTING.

If yours is a classroom where all students have access to a device, you might have smaller study buddy groups, using social media sites like Facebook to share work, explore ideas, review each other's work, and more. Time can be spent learning how to use online social media and chat sites in a thoughtful manner in the safety of the classroom where there will be an adult to act as a guide.

Students can create their own blogs using sites like WordPress. If you go to http://WordPress.com, you will find out how easy it is to set up your own blog. With a blog students can refine their own abilities as a writer as well as share their work within the class. Assignments can be presented as blog posts and in that way they become available to everyone who has access to the blog.

Edmodo (https://www.edmodo.com/) is a safe and easy way to create a digital classroom within which you post assignments and quizzes and provide real-time feedback to students, upload photographs and links to research sites, stay in touch with parents and other teachers, send messages to individual students, and collaborate with people around the world. It is a very useful way to blend technology into the day-to-day learning in the classroom.

If you type "social media in the classroom" into your search engine you will find a wealth of information to provoke your thinking and provide useful ideas about the use of these technologies as a part of learning.

The trick when using any of these forums is to remember to say, "Stop and think about what you are doing before you do it." All of these media are virtually instantaneous. Remember the old saying, "there's many a slip twixt cup and lip?" The space between cup and lip in the digital world is so minute that there is the potential for a lot of spilled tea if we don't learn to stop and think, to manage our impulsivity and communicate with clarity and precision.

It is hard to communicate with clarity or precision when so many of the usual accompaniments to careful communication are missing. Communication is a two-way process—we send and we receive. We can help our children learn how to receive communications from others with clarity and with the expectation of precision. The opportunities for misinterpretation online are enormous and the opportunities to correct misinterpretations are often few and far between.

The Internet is rife with quotations without attribution, facts without substantiation, and opinions hastily reached and widely disseminated. We can read long and heated debates on social media sites that have grown out of an original post based on rumor and innuendo. Choose any contentious political or moral issue and you will find online arguments peppered with misleading information and emotional outbursts. Rarely are they places of clear and precise communication.

Spend some time with your youngsters examining examples of this so that they can build up familiarity with the techniques that are used.

In March 2015, the following post appeared on Facebook:

To Celebrate the Coming of Summer Get 2 Southwest Tickets!
To Get your Tickets, complete the tasks given below:
Task #1. Press "Join" button at the top of the page.
Task #2. Once you join, you will see 'Invite Friends' button, Click the button and select a minimum amount of 100 friends to claim your Tickets.
Get Business Select Tickets if you invite more friends!
Invite 100 friends And Get 1 Ticket (Economy)
Invite 200 friends And Get 2 Tickets (Economy)
Invite 300 friends And Get 1 Ticket (Business Select)
Invite 40 friends And Get 2 Tickets (Business Select) Note: Continuously press TAB & SPACE button to quickly select your friends. Task #3: Write "I Love Summer" in the comments below to show your appreciation.
After confirming you completed the First Two Steps See Instantly if you qualify!

Go Here http://goo.gl/jN82UO

*Note: You MUST complete all the steps or your Tickets will not be valid.

Once you get to the web site you are lured into providing all sorts of information about yourself, which can eventually lead to a wave of telemarketing phone calls and emails—but no free tickets, ever.

Similarly you can go to http://www.snopes.com/info/top25uls.asp and discover the current top 25 urban myths spreading nonsense about everything from onions, to toothpaste and various public figures. Letting your older students explore Snopes is a worthwhile exercise in building an understanding of the dangers of the Internet as an unfiltered source of information. Stop and think.

These Internet scammers and purveyors of false information rely on our inability or unreadiness to seek out clarity and precision in the things we read. Assertions lack precision because they provide no substantiating evidence. The use of overly emotive language clouds our rational judgment, and obscures and gets in the way of precise thinking about the material.

Godwin's Law tells us, "As an online discussion grows longer, the probability of a comparison involving Nazis or Hitler approaches 1." In other words, as online discussions in forums and on social media get longer and longer, the thinking seems to get less and less precise and clear. Eventually the "trump" card is played, and the final insult thrown into the discussion.

Watching this happen as an observer can be amusingly recreational. It can also teach us what to avoid in our own use of language during online discussions. Talk about this with your kids.

This habit of expecting communication to have clarity and precision comes about slowly, as does any habit. As we work with our students we are constantly looking out for ways that help them assess their own communications as well as those of others. The art is in developing the habits of precision and clarity without inhibiting the readiness to use language. Babies learn to talk because they are surrounded by spoken language. Studies of the responses adults make to the early utterances of babies show that very rarely do the adults correct the emerging speech. Instead they tend to elaborate.

When a baby points and excitedly says, "oggie, oggie" as a small pooch passes by, the parent doesn't immediately correct the child with "No dear, it's a dog." Instead the adult is delighted, responsive, and will often extend the language with something like this—"Yes, it's a dog. Isn't he friendly." We aid the development of language by encouraging its use, providing good models, and extending and offering opportunities for youngsters to extend their own language. Think back to the section of the book where we explored the power of questions to deepen thought—pause, paraphrase, and probe.

When we begin to appreciate the value of clear and precise communication in our lives we begin to value the behaviors that bring it about. When we see those behaviors as valuable we are more inclined to exercise the habits. By helping our children to understand which web sites can be trusted as authorities and which cannot, by encouraging them to look for verification of statements that seem too good, too bad, or just too outlandish to be true, we are helping them be precise and clear recipients of communication. As Abraham Lincoln is reported to have said, "You can't trust everything you read on the Internet."

THINKING INTERDEPENDENTLY

Perhaps one of the thinking behaviors or Habits of Mind that is most powerfully supported by the Internet is the opportunity to share knowledge and ideas with others. There are forums online for almost every interest, from quantum mechanics to photography, from cooking to the raising of lizards. People in these forums are eager to both share their own knowledge and experiences and to learn from others.

While there is a multitude of forums available for adults there are many for kids too and a simple Google search will uncover them. At this time www.Kidzworld.com, http://community.scholastic.com/all-kids-boards.html, and http://forums.gardenweb.com/forums/teach offer a range of topics including school and homework help, health advice, music, sports, and even politics and religion. Young writers gain access to a wide range of online resources at http://study.com/articles/40_of_the_Best_Websites_for_Young_Writers.html. Usually all that is required is a simple registration process. As time goes by, these web sites come and go, but a search engine will always winkle out the latest ones.

Don't forget to engage with children about their discussions and the things they are discovering on the forums they use. You can always check that the forums have robust safeguards in place. These should include the monitoring of chat rooms and postings by actual people as well as sophisticated software. You can check out the safety procedures by reviewing the home page or by scrolling to the bottom of the home page. If there is no safety protocol in place you should be very diligent in supervising access by younger children. The world of the Internet is a broad country and there are many travelers within it, many beautiful landscapes, and some dangerous dark alleys.

There is a wealth of programs available to enable students to collaborate with others in the same classroom or in other parts of the world. They can work and think interdependently as they seek out information, as they explore what they have found out and begin to integrate it into what they already know and as they find ways to present their findings to others. They can produce documents together, adding and editing together, browse web sites simultaneously with others, create collaborative mind maps, watch videos together and chat online about what they have seen, draw and sketch, adding to one another's images, and more. Web sites tend to come and go but a search engine will provide a wealth of suggestions if you simply type in "collaborative software for students."

One very useful site can be found here: http://www.educatorstechnology.com/2012/08/the-top-27-free-tools-to-collaborate.html; and it provides links to twenty-seven different online collaboration tools for use inside the classroom.

KEY IDEAS IN THIS CHAPTER

- Our young people need to be life ready as well as college and career ready.
- Certain kinds of behaviors support deep water thinking and they are described by the Habits of Mind.
- Some of these Habits of Mind are particularly valuable in developing deeper thinking in this digital age:
  - *Persisting*—requires focus, having a variety of strategies, being able to evaluate
  - *Managing impulsivity*—be able to detach, slow down, think deeply, planning helps as does the careful use of questioning, and withholding of judgment
  - *Communicating with clarity and precision*—taking the time to use precise and appropriate language and knowing and applying the rules that govern that language. Online scammers rely on our failure to read carefully with an expectation of clarity and precision from others
  - *Thinking interdependently*—the Internet is a powerful force for this Habit of collaboration.

DISCUSSION

- For a behavior to become a habit we need to see the value in repeating it, until it becomes an automatic part of the way we operate in the world. What can you do in your school or classroom to help students see the value of these Habits of Mind in their own lives?

- Describe some different kinds of situations where persistence was demonstrated. Can you find any elements that are common to them all and make it possible to persist?
- What do you see as the link between impulsivity and creativity?
- Does managing impulsivity mean limiting creativity?
- How do you encourage clarity and precision in students' oral language without inhibiting their readiness to speak?

Chapter Fourteen

Am I Clever Enough to Think in the Deep End?

It is easy to come to the conclusion that our society doesn't really expect everyone to be a deep thinker, and that most of us are only safe in the shallows and it is probably best that we remain there. The superficial nature of many news reports and the kinds of programs that flourish on our televisions seem more inclined to keep us amused rather than make us think.

But the fact is that we can all become deeper-water thinkers.

There is another perhaps unexpected factor involved in helping our youngsters to become deeper thinkers. It too comes from our growing understanding about the plasticity of the human brain. It used to be the accepted wisdom that at some time in early adulthood our brains had matured and reached their optimum state. From that time onwards we would find ourselves in an inevitable state of gradual cerebral decline and decay. One of the consequences of this mechanistic view of the brain—that it is a kind of machine that once fully built can only then gradually wear out—was that we thought of intelligence as some kind of fixed quantity.

IQ TESTS

Intelligence testing began at the beginning of the twentieth century when a French psychologist, Alfred Binet, designed the first tests for the French government in order to identify those students who might have difficulties at school. This was during the time when French children were first required to attend school. Although Binet insisted on the complexity of intelligence and argued that it was too wide ranging to be measured with any single measure, the test he devised became the foundation for all subsequent IQ tests.

During World War I, IQ tests were used widely in the United States initially to screen army recruits, but soon to be used in a wide variety of contexts. Binet's test and a later one devised by the American psychologist Arnold Weschler can still be found in updated forms in a variety of institutions today, including our schools. The acceptance into Gifted Education programs is often based on an IQ score as well as other measures.

The problem with IQ tests is that their users have developed a kind of built-in assumption about them, that IQ is a fixed measurement. The average IQ is 100 and many countries define significant mental disability as being demonstrated by an IQ below 70. In some states of the USA a convicted criminal cannot be executed if he or she has an IQ below 70.

In 2002, in the case *Atkins v. Virginia* the Supreme Court ruled that it violated the eighth Amendment ban on "cruel and unusual punishment" to execute a person with "mental retardation." In various states of the USA mental retardation is defined as having an IQ below 70 together with significant deficits in adaptive behavior. In other words, we have come to define people in part by their IQ and a man with a measured IQ of 65 may not be executed whereas a man with a measured IQ of 70 may.

But intelligence is not fixed and the brain is not a static entity.

The brain is in a constant state of flux and change. The brain you had when you began to read this book is not the same as the brain you have now. We are constantly making and unmaking new connections between our more than one hundred billion neurons. Neurons are pruned and new ones are made throughout our lives. Each neuron has a multitude of branching dendrites that make contact with the dendrites of other neurons.

These points of contact are called synapses and there are one hundred billion of synapses inside our brains. As we sense things, experience things, think things, and learn things, there is a complex exchange of neurochemical signals at these synapses and this is how neural pathways are formed. When the same neural pathway is used repeatedly it becomes more and more defined. Donald Hebb, a Canadian psychologist, wrote a book in 1949 titled "The Organization of Behavior" in which he described the behavior of neurons during learning. His findings came to be known as Hebb's Law— "neurons that fire together wire together."

With the use of functional magnetic resonance imaging we are now able to actually watch these neurons firing as they show up as "hot spots" of brain activity on a screen. Every experience creates new and different neural pathways and we can continue to develop these new pathways into very old age. Learning new and challenging things is the best way to encourage the development of strong, new neural pathways.

THE PLASTIC BRAIN AND MINDSET

Two fascinating books that will give a great deal of information and case studies based on the concept brain plasticity are Norman Doidge's book "The Brain That Changes Itself" (Doidge, 2007) and Ramachandran's book "The Tell Tale Brain" (Ramachandran, 2011).

An important corollary of this new view of the brain as plastic and constantly capable of new learning and change is the awareness that given the right circumstances, most of us can learn most things. It is simply not good enough to say, for example, that a girl will never be able to do mathematics because it's hard for girls, or because her mother was hopeless at math.

The phrase "I can't do that" needs to be replaced with the phrase "I can't do that yet." There is little real basis for dividing our children up into those who are good with their brains and those who are good with their hands. They can all be good with their brains given the right *mindset*.

The notion of mindset has been brought to our notice largely by a professor of psychology at Stanford University, Carol Dweck. In her book (Dweck, 2006) she describes her work with some of her own students. Dweck postulated that there are two basic mindsets—a fixed mindset and a growth mindset. A person with a fixed mindset believes that their intelligence is fixed, that it is a part of who they are as a person. The growth mindset person believes that intelligence is something that can be developed through effort, that how clever they are depends not on who they are, but on what they do.

Dweck carried out a very simple, but a very revealing study. She took two groups of low achieving seventh-grade mathematics students and gave each of them a set of identical classes on study skills. One of the groups was given some additional lessons on memory and study skills while the second group was given some simple information about the plasticity of their brains and she explained to them that with effort even things that were very hard could be achieved because the brain is like a muscle, it gets stronger with more work. The students were then randomly placed in mathematics groups for the rest of the school term, without identifying them to their teachers.

When they sat for their final exams there was a significant difference in performance between the students who had been in each of the two groups. The study skills and memory group had made no improvement at all, whereas the growth mindset group had made significant progress and teachers commented on their motivation to learn.

The essential difference between the two groups was the belief among the members of one group that ability came from effort, and that hard work was what made intelligent, successful problem-solvers and thinkers, not just natural ability.

What does this mean for us in developing metacognitive thinkers?

Thinking can be hard work, and, sadly, in our society it is all too easy for some of our children to be led to believe that they were just not up to it. If we expect our children to be prepared to stop and think about what they are doing, what they are reading and being told, about what they believe and value, then we have to ensure that they believe thinking is something at which they can succeed, even excel.

The ever-increasing regime of testing in schools is reaching further and further into early childhood. With every test comes another opportunity for success ... and failure. If there is a lot riding on success in a test and a child doesn't do well, they can soon begin to see themselves as not very clever and here lie the beginnings of the fixed mindset: I can't do well in tests → I'm not good at tests → I'm not good at school → I'm not very clever.

In another of Carol Dweck's experiments she took two groups of students and gave them each a test. It was fairly easy so they all did reasonably well. With one group she made comments to students along these lines, "you must be very clever to do so well," "you must be quite intelligent," "I expected you to do well because you have a high IQ," and the like. The second group of students was told something quite different. When she spoke to them she said things like "You must have tried very hard in that test" and "I could see you were not going to give up."

The students were then asked to do a second test, but they were given a choice. They could choose to do a test that was harder than the one they had just done, or they could do one that was easier. Significantly more of the students in the first group who had a fixed mindset reinforced by Dweck chose to do the easier test, and more of the students in the second group who had a growth mindset reinforced chose the harder one.

If we focus on effort rather than native ability, people are more prepared to take on difficult challenges.

THE PRAISE PROBLEM

What does this mean for how we interact with our children and young people? We need to make sure that our children understand that we love them for who they are—unconditionally, but that we praise them for what they do.

Consider this. You have an adorable little two-year-old girl. She has big, soft brown eyes, crinkly curls that frame her face, a smile that makes her nose wrinkle in a way that melts your heart. You look at her with all the love you have shining on your face; you sweep her into your arms saying "What a cute kid you are with those big brown eyes. I love you so much."

Let's go back, for a moment, to Skinner's conditioning. Your two-year-old is making a powerful connection between your words, your actions, and your obvious love for her—"I am cute and you love me." This is such a short step from, "You love me because I am cute." In a classical stimulus response fashion she comes to see love as being stimulated by being cute. If this is reinforced throughout her early childhood, what might happen?

Pat recalls walking around the playground of her school at the end of the school day when the class photographs had been handed out to be taken home. She saw one little third grader sitting on a seat under a tree, sobbing. Her photos were in her hand. She sat down next to her and asked her what was wrong. She seemed so sad. Between her tears she told me, "I'm not cute any more." She was right. She had reached that gangly age, where her features hadn't quite sorted out their dominance on a face that has lost its baby softness. Her arms and legs were a bit too long for her body, rather like a foal's.

What saddened her was that she valued herself according to some scale of cuteness, and she felt she had suddenly slipped. Did she believe that being cute was the foundation for being loved? What would she feel about herself when she hit thirteen and faced the twin horrors of zits and either an over- or underdeveloped bosom? We need to think very carefully about the kind of praise we give to children.

We have far too many gifted children who become school failures and dropouts in adolescence. Why does this happen? We have watched gifted children who find every academic task they are given at school to be a breeze. They are never really challenged and they always seem to get A grades and ten out of ten on tests. Everyone knows they are the clever ones in the class because it is all so easy. When they bring home a report card emblazoned with As at the end of term their parents are proud and tell them so. "How clever you are for getting those marks" they say, in so many words.

Later, in secondary school, the work starts to get a bit more challenging. The depth of thinking and the amount of effort required rise dramatically. It's no longer a matter of being able to spell twenty words, complete a picture and words project on Egypt, or do a page of arithmetic. Now it's the analysis of Shakespearean tragedy, metaphysical poetry, logarithms, and the Laws of Thermodynamics. This is real work. Effort is not something they know a lot about. It is certainly not something they have had to factor into their school experience in any significant way. They have never had to struggle and perhaps ... heaven forbid ... fail. They have not needed to develop the resilience that comes from facing failing but trying again.

To make matters worse, they have come to believe that their parents and teachers are proud of them because they get As, because they are clever. Being a clever student who always gets As is who they are. What will happen to their parents' love if they only get a C or worse still, fail? If this attitude is coupled to a fixed mindset—that this C-level performance is the best I can do, that I have reached the limit of my ability, then there is no motivation to keep trying. For too many this is too great a risk to take. Better by far not to take the risk, not to try, to refuse the task, not turn up, drop out. The other alternative taken by some is to fail so brilliantly that everyone will know they didn't take the task seriously, didn't care.

The additional layer of complexity here is that all these tend to happen at a time when these kids are at their most vulnerable—early adolescence. This is a time when the sense of self is fragile and the opinions of others become gold. It's a time for challenging parents and seeking out the boundaries of their love and tolerance.

I ALSO LOVE THE WAY YOU THINK

We are not suggesting for a moment that loving parents should not acknowledge their toddler's cuteness or be overtly proud of their child's report card. What is important is that your children know that your love is unconditional, that you, like every parent, think they are the most amazing, beautiful children in the world, but that you also value even more than their cuteness or grades, the amount of hard work they are prepared to put into things.

Your daughter needs to know that you think she is beautiful, but also that you value her ability to stick to her principles, to struggle with a difficult task, to show empathy toward others, to get on with her playmates, to be curious about the world, to bounce back and try again when she fails, and so on. Little by little she needs to come to understand that she cannot take credit for the things she didn't earn—her big brown eyes, her top marks in a test for which she didn't need to study.

DEEP THINKING MAKES BRAINS GROW, EVEN WHEN WE FAIL

Hopefully she will also learn that every time she struggles with something difficult she is making her brain grow, in a very real and physical sense. She is creating new neural pathways and increasing the amazing complexity of her brain. Hopefully too, our brightest children will be offered the privilege of failing because they have been asked to do something that is a little too hard when first attempted. Their experience of struggle will teach them about resilience, about the need to think flexibly and look for alternative solutions to problems, and the value of working interdependently with others who may know something more. They will learn too that the world values effort and their sense of self-worth will grow as they demonstrate their ability to overcome difficulties.

Consider the school where the usual awards for academic excellence were given out at the end of the year, but there was also a prize for something that isn't often acknowledged. This school would obtain two new, shiny bicycles and helmets each year. Teachers would be asked to nominate children in their year levels who had shown grit and determination to bring up their grades. These were not the children who got As or even Bs. Sometimes a child might be nominated who had pulled a failing grade up to a C.

What was important was the demonstration of effort. It may have puzzled some of the children who had consistently achieved As and only got a certificate or at best, a book, to see that a child with Cs was getting a bicycle. Some of the teachers had a hard time putting aside the habits of many years and congratulating not just the children with the highest grades, but also the children who had put in effort. But the school persisted with this because they wanted to make it absolutely clear that what they valued even more highly than an easily gained A was a hard-won B. They valued effort, and thinking is always hard work.

We are all clever enough to think in the deep end.

This interconnected, dynamic electronic world is filled with fascination and distraction. Its bright lights, its sounds, and its demands for our attention envelope us all day and every day. Some of us even sleep with our smartphones beside us on the bedside table, waking up for each "plink" indicating a new Facebook post, tweet, or email message.

We have even invented a new word to describe this state of constant connection—"fomo"—the fear of missing out. The Internet has an unimaginable capacity to connect us with each other and it makes a fathomless pool of knowledge and information available to us in an instant. It can spin us around, swirling us inside a heady environment of more and more and more information, until we are dizzy and unable to think.

A salutary lesson can be had from following an argument on a social forum such as Facebook. You read something that sparks your interest and so you respond. You know the person who posted the comment that caught your eye, but you have no idea who the person is who responds to your remark. Then a third person chimes in, and a fourth and a fifth. Then we are back to the third person, before another wild card enters. Typically there is little thought, a great deal of impulsive responsiveness, and, not infrequently, some personal abuse. Then someone posts a link to an online blog where a person totally unknown to anyone previously offers their opinion, together with claims and statements that can be neither sourced nor verified. All of this happens at almost breathtaking speed.

It's fun to go with the flow, to avoid the hard work, the *thinking* work. But we are in danger of becoming uncritical consumers of information rather than thinkers, because we are so enmeshed in this dynamic, ubiquitous networked world. We risk splashing about in the shallow end of thought, bewitched by the flashes of light and the beautiful patterns and colors that decorate the surface. It's easy to stay in the shallows, but splashing about in the shallows is unlikely to provide opportunities for the effort that encourages a growth mindset.

> We create new neural pathways and more complex and intelligent brains, when we struggle with difficult problems and search for new solutions, when we master new skills. This can only happen when we disentangle ourselves for a while from the fascinating, ever-changing, dynamic shallow end, and when we think *deliberately* and *metacognitively*.

We need to learn how to dive deeper, to slow down, and to look more closely and in more detail at less. We must teach our children how to discover the richness of the depths as well as well as appreciating the delights of the surface.

Deep water thinking is more profound thinking, and it is the kind of thinking that will help ensure our children are able to function optimally in this fast-moving world, able to understand, and keep themselves safe from the currents and the undertows and not simply be swept along and away by them.

Only a student with a growth mindset will be prepared to take the risks and enter the deeper waters of more profound thinking. They are not afraid of temporary failures and missteps—in fact they expect them and sometimes welcome them. They know they may have to ask for a helping hand from time to time when the currents are sweeping them along or when they lose their footing.

But that doesn't bother a student with a growth mindset because there is the awareness that learning is a risk-taking business. A student with a growth mindset is able to embrace the gamble of possible failure because his sense of worth is not tied up with success, but it is tied up with effort.

KEY IDEAS IN THIS CHAPTER

- IQ testing was based on a false assumption—that once the brain had finished growing we were pretty much stuck with the intelligence we had at that time.
- We know that this is not the case. Our brains are plastic and change with every new experience.
- Carol Dweck noticed that students with a fixed mindset (those who believed that their intelligence was fixed) tended to avoid difficult tasks, whereas those with a growth mindset (those who believed that they could improve their intelligence by trying hard tasks) were prepared to challenge themselves.
- In studies the students with the growth mindset did better in tests than those with the fixed mindset.
- The growth mindset focuses on effort. We must be careful about the things we praise in children.
- Many gifted children drop out or deliberately fail because their self-image is tied to a fixed view of their intelligence and failure would risk the loss of this.
- Trying to learn anything difficult causes the brain to make new connections between neurons.

DISCUSSION

- Have you ever learned something that at first you thought was impossible for you to master? What were some of the factors that enabled your eventual success?
- What ways do you have to recognize effort rather than achievement with students?
- Can you identify anyone—within or outside the school—who you would describe as having either a growth or a fixed mindset? How can you tell?
- How do you ensure that students in your care feel safe enough to take risks in their learning? What do you see as the main obstacles to their productive risk taking?
- What techniques do you use to disentangle from the frantic pace of daily and digital life in order to think in depth?

Conclusion

In this book we have explored the ways in which electronic media have changed and continue to change the world and the ways in which we think.

We have focused on two kinds of thinking. One is linear and the other is networked. We hope that we have demonstrated the need to become skilled in both.

We have taken a journey through the growing understanding of how we learn and what we mean by "education" and we have examined the implications of incorporating technology into the Common Core State Standards (CCSS).

We have considered the problems of the digital divide and examined the importance of the adults coming to understand the world within which young people live so that they can behave like adults and provide youngsters with the tools they need to navigate this new landscape.

We have considered ways in which we can practically help our young people to disentangle from the network long enough to focus and think more deeply about problems and to come to understand how they do the most important task of their lives—thinking.

In particular we hope we have demonstrated the importance of teaching our young people how to think in the deep end and we have provided practical strategies in line with the CCSS that you can implement in your school or classroom.

We have covered a great expanse together and explored a vast, often unfamiliar, ocean and reminisced about some old more familiar haunts. We have splashed about in the shallows as well as venturing into some pretty deep water. We hope that you have enjoyed the trip and perhaps understand a little more about the world within which our children will spend their lives.

We have tried to provide a bridge of understanding between the print-oriented, linear worlds of the past and the networked, dynamic world of the digital age.

Hopefully we have persuaded you that everyone can become a deeper thinker and that some particular behaviors will help us along the way if we practice them, become proficient with them, and choose to use them.

Above all we hope we have provided a convincing argument about why the grown-ups need to stay in charge as their children carry out their own explorations. We must provide the support our youngsters need until they are skilled and confident enough to swim alone. We need to lead them safely out of the shallows and into the deep end of the ocean.

> We shall not cease from exploration, and the end of all our exploring will be to arrive where we started and know the place for the first time.
>
> —T S Elliot, Four Quartets

Bibliography

American Academy of Child and Adolescent Psychiatry (AACAP), "Facts for Families Guide", retrieved from https://www.aacap.org/AACAP/Families_and_Youth/Facts_for_Families/FFF-Guide/Children-And-Watching-TV-054.aspx, 2015.

Australian Communications and Media Authority (ACMA), "Children's Television Viewing, Research Overview", retrieved from http://www.acma.gov.au/~/media/Research%20and%20Analysis/Research/pdf/OverviewChildrens%20television%20viewingFinal%20pdf.pdf), 2015.

Berninger, V. "Evidence-Based, Developmentally Appropriate Writing Skills K–5: Teaching the Orthographic Loop of Working Memory to Write Letters So Developing Writers Can Spell Words and Express Ideas." Presented at Handwriting in the 21st Century?: An Educational Summit, Washington, DC, January 23, 2012.

Carr, N. *The Shallows: What the Internet Is Doing to Our Brains"* Norton & Co., New York City, New York, USA, 2010.

Chomsky, N. *Syntactic Structures*. Walter de Gruyter, Berlin, Germany, 2002.

Common Core Standards (CCS), retrieved from http://www.corestandards.org/what-parents-should-know/, 2009.

Costa, A. and B. Kallick. *Leading and Learning With Habits of Mind: 16 Essential Characteristics for Success*. Association for Supervision and Curriculum Development, Alexandria, Virginia, USA, 2008.

Coviello, L., Y. Sohn, A.D.I. Kramer, C. Marlow, M. Franceschetti, N.A. Christakis, and J.H. Fowler. "Detecting Emotional Contagion in Massive Social Networks." *PloS One* 9, no. 3: e90315. 2014.

Doidge, N. *The Brain That Changes Itself: Stories of Personal Triumph from the Frontiers of Brain Science*. Viking Penguin, New York City, New York, USA, 2007.

Dweck, C. *Mindset: The New Psychology of Success*. Ballantine Books, New York City, New York, USA, 2006.

Godin, S. Retrieved from http://www.sethgodin.com/sg/docs/StopStealingDreamsSCREEN.pdf or https://www.youtube.com/watch?v=sXpbONjV1Jc, 2012.

Growing Up Digital (GUD). Retrieved from http://philmcrae.com/blog.html, November 28, 2016.

James, K.H. and L. Engelhardt. "The Effects of Handwriting Experience on Functional Brain Development in Pre-literate Children." *Trends in Neuroscience and Education* 1, no. 1: 32–42. 2012.

Kraushaar, J.M. and D.C. Novak. "Examining the Effects of Student Multitasking With Laptops During the Lecture." *Journal of Information Systems Education* 21, no. 2: 241–251. 2010.

Marzano, R. *Classroom Instruction That Works: Research Based Strategies for Increasing Student Achievement.* Association for Supervision and Curriculum Development, Alexandria, Virginia, USA, 2001.

McLuhan, M. and Q. Fiore. *The Medium Is the Massage: an Inventory of Effects.* Gingko Press, Berkley, California, USA, 9th edition, 2001.

Medimorec, S. and E.F. Risko. "Effects of Disfluency in Writing." *Canada British Journal of Psychology.* Published online 20th January, 2016.

Mueller, P.A. and D.M. Oppenheimer. "The Pen Is Mightier Than the Keyboard: Advantages of Longhand Over Laptop Note Taking." *Psychological Science*, Sage, 2014.

National Education Technology Plan (NETP). Retrieved from http://tech.ed.gov/netp/. 2016.

National Research Council (NRC). "Developing Transferable Knowledge and Skills in the 21st Century." In J.W. Pellegrino and M.L. Hilton, editors. National Academies Press, Washington, DC, USA, 2012.

Oxford Mindfulness Centre (OMC). Retrieved from http://oxfordmindfulness.org/. 2016.

Pew Research Center's Internet & American Life Project survey. Retrieved from www.pewinternet.org/files/old-media/Files/.../PIP_Digital_differences_041312.pdf, 2011.

Prensky, M. "Digital Natives to Digital Wisdom." Corwin, Thousand Oaks, California, USA, 2012.

Ramachandran, V.M. *The Tell-Tale Brain: A Neuroscientist's Quest for What Makes Us Human.* Norton, New York City, New York, USA, 2011.

Robinson, K. *Out of Our Minds: Learning to be Creative.* Capstone, Hoboken, New Jersey, USA, 2011.

Robinson, K. *Finding Your Element: How to Discover Your Talents and Passions and Transform Your Life.* Viking Penguin, New York City, New York, USA, 2013.

Suzuki, S. (translated by W. Suzuki). *Nurtured by Love. A New Approach to Education.* New York Exposition Press, New York City, New York, USA, 1969.

University of Massachusetts Medical School, Center for Mindfulness (UMMS). Retrieved from http://www.umassmed.edu/cfm/

Wagner, T. *The Global Achievement Gap: Why Even Our Best Schools Don't Teach the New Survival Skills Our Children Need—and What We Can Do About It.* Basic Books, Perseus Book Group, New York City, New York, USA, 2008. See also http://www.tonywagner.com/7-survival-skills.

FURTHER READING

Arbesman, S. *Let's Bring the Polymath – and the Dabbler – Back.* (*Wired* 12/13/13).
Bronson, P.O. and A. Merryman. *Nurture Shock*, Twelve, Hachette Book Group, New York City, New York, USA, 2009.
Christakis, A. and F. Zimmerman. *The Elephant in the Living Room: Make Television Work for your Kids.* Rodale, Distributed to the book trade by Holtzbrinck Publishers New York City, New York, USA, 2006.
Gladwell, M. *Outliers.* Hachette, Book Group, New York City, New York, USA, 2008.
Greenfield, S. *Mind Change: How Digital Technologies Are Leaving Their Mark on Our Brains.* Random House, New York City, New York, USA, 2015.
How People Learn – Bridging Research and Practice. National Research Council, National Academies Press, Washington, DC, USA, 1999.
How People Learn: Brain, Mind, Experience and School. National Research Council, National Academies Press, Washington, DC, USA, 2000.
How Students Learn: History, Mathematics and Science in the Classroom. National Research Council, National Academies Press, Washington, DC, USA, 2005.
Mitra, S. "Beyond the Hole in the Wall: Discover the Power of Self-Organized Learning." TED Conferences, Retrieved from https:/www.youtube.com/watch?v=HE5GX3U3BYQ, 2012.
O'Shae, M. *The Brain: a Very Short Introduction.* Oxford University Press, Oxford, UK, 2005.
Pinker, S. *"How the Mind Works."* W.W. Norton, New York City, New York, USA, 1997.
Preparing Teachers: Building Evidence for Sound Policy. National Research Council, National Academies Press, Washington, DC, USA, 2010.
Wagner, T. *The Global Achievement Gap: Why Even Our Best Schools Don't Teach the New Survival Skills Our Children Need—and What We Can Do About It.* Basic Books, 2010.

Index

adaptability, 45
Age of Reason. *See* Renaissance
analogies, teachers utilizing, 27
Arab Spring, 99
Arbesman, Samuel, 18
Aristotle, 14, 17
artificial intelligence, 61
assembly line: core of, 52; development of, 20–21; education as, 21
attitude, 141

balance, 75, 79–80, 87
behaviorism, 32–33
behaviors: children learning, 100; context provided by, 160; deep thinking influenced by, 160–61; development of, 5; as impulsive, 166; problems with, 167
Benz, Karl, 5
Bernstein, Basil, 39
Beyond the Hole in the Wall (Mitra), 108
Bible, 17
binary thinking, 89, 90–92
Binet, Alfred, 175
block scheduling, 2
Bloom, Benjamin: influence of, 153; taxonomy of, 35, 38, 150

brain: activations in, 91; of children, 61; as constantly changing, 176; deeper thinking allowing growth in, 180–82; development of, 2, 61, 138; Internet similar to, 21; mechanistic view of, 175; as most important tool, 133; as network, 61; as non linear, 60; plasticity of, 84, 104, 177–78; world and, 21–22
The Brain that Changes Itself (Doidge), 104, 177
Bruner, Jerome, 38
bullying, 98; as cruel, 100; exclusion as form of, 101

Cambourne, Brian, 34
Carr, Nicholas, 154
Catch 22 (Heller), 16
CCSS. *See* Common Core State Standards
character education, 3
cheating, 152
childhood, values, obedience and, 62
children: abstract thinking of, 36; attention of, 138; behavior taught to, 100; beliefs of, 127; brains of, 61; conditioning for, 33; control for, 97; in digital age, 4, 23; direct experience as critical for, 78–79; effective thinking

for, 43; effort demonstrated by, 181;
as empowered, 8; encouragement for,
65, 167; engaging of, 172; exclusion
of, 99; experience influencing, 57, 122;
failure of, 52; as gifted, 179; gossip of,
115; habits of, 44; as hypersensitive,
144; imagination for, 51; impulsivity
in, 169; as independent learners,
68, 131, 138; as interrogated, 144;
language abilities of, 34, 56, 114;
literacy levels of, 4; metacognition
of, 142, 149; opportunities for,
8–9; parent assistance for, 46, 64,
186; as persistent, 84; praise for,
178; punishments for, 33; questions
benefitting, 66; rage in, 77; relating as
useful for, 55; responsibility learned
by, 103; rewards for, 33; rules for, 72,
112; safety for, 95; selectivity learned
by, 123; speaking learned by, 104;
teacher assistance for, 46; television
use of, 71; as threatened, 140; tools for,
72, 127; as trapped, 2; as valued, 141;
websites suitable for, 121–22; words
utilized by, 137; worldview of, 51
Chomsky, Noam, 34, 39
Clark, Lane, 38
classrooms: as busy, 140; collaboration
in, 173; as digital, 169; as factories,
50–52; as flipped, 3; physical
experiences in, 78; survival struggle
in, 11; technology in, 96
climate change, 5
cognitive skills, 44
cognitivism, 33–35
Common Core State Standards (CCSS),
3, 50, 159; argument skills standard
of, 120; communication standards of,
101, 167–68; design of, 45; digital
media explored by, 70; experiments
promoted by, 78; goals for, 143;
mathematics standards of, 142–43,
163; purpose of, 143; standards for,
24; technology in, 6, 96, 185; writing
standards of, 89, 123

communication: art of, 87; CCSS
standards for, 102, 167–68; chatting
as form of, 81; as clear, 167–72; as
effective, 45; as face-to-face, 101;
nonverbal aspects of, 81; power
of, 101–2; process of, 170; reading
replacing, 69; student standards for,
6; as thoughtful, 144
competition, 108
Concrete Operational Stage, 36
conditioning, 33
constructivism, 2; argument for, 35–36;
learning according to, 40
cooperative learning, 2
core knowledge, 2
corporal punishment, 62
Costa, Arthur, 8, 39, 56, 65, 135, 160
creative thinking, 2; encouraging of, 56;
process of, 153; for students, 50; as
valued, 21
critical thinking, 2, 45
curriculum: change in, 124–25; focus of,
6; shift away from, 36; for teachers,
51; writing in, 90
cursive writing, 89
cyber safety, 97, 112

dating websites: as dangerous, 103;
virtual power of, 79
da Vinci, Leonardo, 14, *15*, 18
deep thinking, 131; behaviors influencing,
159–60; binary thinking compared
to, 89; brain growth through, 180–82;
capacity for, 175, 181; as critical, 168;
about digital media, 112; disconnection
important for, 118; encouraging of,
135, 185; metacognition as, 134–36;
as practiced, 175; as profound, 182;
questions encouraged by, 128; safety
necessary for, 95; for search engines
use, 122; skills for, 153; skimming
debilitating, 137; by slowing down,
92–93, 117; as successful, 159–60;
from television, 71; tools for,
134, 166

depression, 85
Dewey, John, 38
Dewey decimal system, 12, 120
Diamond, Jared, 18
digital age: change from, 72; children in, 4, 23; contributors in, 53–54; dangers of, 155; as dynamic, 186; education, learning and, 29; globalization in, 11; preparation for, 49; skills in, 64; thinking changed by, 7; value of, 79–80
digital dementia, 163
digital devices: addiction to, 163; children rules for, 113; etiquette for use of, 114; instructions for, 108
digital divide, 59–60, 185
digital immigrants, 59
digital media: as captivating, 60; CCSS exploring, 70; change from, 185; deep thinking about, 112; linear thinking removed by, 104
digital natives, 59
digital printer, 21
digital world: balance in, 75; dating in, 102–3; disconnection in, 80–81; as distracting, 86; interconnection through, 76; living in, 7; as ocean, 1; reality in, 76–77, 80; as resource, 78–79; as seductive, 76; socialization in, 77; surface thinking and, 81–82; tangible world interactions with, 75–76, 77, 79, 81
Diigo, 20
disconnection, 80–81
distraction, 154
diversity, 52–55
Doidge, Norman, 104, 177
Dropbox, 118
Dweck, Carol, 39, 177, 178

education: as assembly line, 21; defining of, 29; digital age, learning and, 29; historical transformations in, 30; inadequacy in, 52; meaning of, 185; model of, 21; reading as focus for, 17; reform of, 72; of thinking and feeling, 101; twenty-first century tasks for, 127; understanding of, 2, 28, 40; as utilitarian, 30; for women, 29
Einstein, Albert, 13; knowledge opinion of, 128–29; talents of, 18
Einstein and the Poet: In Search of Cosmic Man (Hermanns), 128
Elaboration Theory, 35
electronic media. *See* digital media
e-mail, 118–19
emotions: learning influenced by, 153; timing influenced by, 148
engagement: change increasing, 85; of children, 172; as face-to-face, 168; from parents, 1; of students, 100; with tangible world, 77, 84; from teachers, 1; texting decreasing, 113
entrepreneurship, 45
esteem, 37
ethics, 152
evaluation, 152–153

Facebook, 22, 71, 126; group rules for, 169; influence of, 77; popularity of, 115; as powerful medium, 82
family: influence of, 39; as interactive, 70; values transmitted from, 63
fight or flight, 141
flexibility, 132
Formal Operational Stage, 36
Fowler, John, 22

Galileo, 18
games: learning debilitated by, 83; as strategic, 165–66; as valuable, 83
Gardner, Howard, 39
Genghis Khan, 20
gist thinking, 154
Gi-won, Byun, 163
Gladwell, Malcolm, 54
Global Financial Crisis, 22
globalization, 11
Godin, Seth, 54
Godwin's Law, 171

Google, 19, 54, 120–21, 126; as not enough, 129; teaching beyond, 123
Great Horse Manure Crisis, 5

Habits of Mind, 3, 65, 160–61; examples of, 161; Internet supporting, 172
Hanauma Bay, 1
handwriting: individuality proclaimed by, 90; memory increased by, 91; teaching of, 89; typing compared to, 92
Hebb, Donald, 176
Hebb's Law, 176
Heller, Joseph, 16
Hermanns, William, 128
hierarchy of human needs, of Maslow, 31
humanism, 37
human race: challenges of, 5; gift for, 8; history of, 5; media influencing, 22; needs for, 37
hyperlinks, 137–38, 154

imagination, 46, 51
immigrants, 63, 64
improvisation, 24
impulsivity: as behavioral, 166; in children, 169; creativity in, 166; managing of, 165–67, 169; social media encouraging, 117
Industrial Revolution, 21, 30, 31
Inquisition, 17
integrated curriculum, 3
INTEL, 23
interconnection: through digital world, 76; of Internet, 20; through television, 71
Internet: beliefs created by, 127; brain similar to, 21; change from, 18–20; as city, 109; as collaborative, 7; as dangerous, 96; as exciting, 4; false information on, 171; Habits of Mind supported by, 172; information searching through, 19; interconnectivity of, 20; as limitless, 131; navigating of, 155; as not clear, 170; opinions found on, 149; as reward, 114; as rumor mill, 120; in tangible world, 77–78; thinking produced by, 133; updating of, 61
interpersonal skills, 44
intrapersonal skills, 44
intuition: as accepted, 22; as fact, 128; musicians using, 14; as suspicious, 12; as valued, 24
IQ tests, 175–77

James, Clive, 119

Kallick, Bena, 39, 65, 135, 160
Kierkegaard, Soren, 159
knowledge, 2, 128–29; explosion of, 12; importance of, 44; preserving of, 17; sharing of, 172; transferring of, 133

Labov, William, 39
leadership, 44
Leading and Learning with Habits of the Mind (Costa and Kallick), 135
learning: as complex, 2, 34; constructivism view of, 40; digital age, education and, 29; as dynamic, 83; emotions influenced by, 153; through experience, 83; games debilitating, 83; of immigrants, 63; integration in, 19; as limitless, 131; as non linear, 40; through observing, 80; organizational structure of, 35; playing as tool for, 107; about privacy settings, 115; responsibility of, 57; science of, 30–40; of senses, 84; stages of, 36; as taught, 133; teaching compared to, 35; theories of, 28, 40; types of, 3; understanding of, 32, 40–41; of values, 62, 63; views of, 37–40; of vocabulary, 139
libraries: change in, 19; digital availability in, 22
Lincoln, Abraham (President), 119

linear thinking, 11–14; digital media removing, 104; as powerful, 24; as skill, 64; striving for, 14
literacy, 69; children levels of, 4; flowering of, 17; as focus, 49
Luther, Martin, 17

Madison, Dolly, 55
magnetic resonance imaging, 60, 128, 176
manners: in digital world, 99–101; for smart phones, 100
Marzano, Robert, 27
Maslow, Abraham, 31, *37*, 50
mathematics, 124, 142, 163
McIntosh, Ewan, 123
McLuhan, Marshall, 11
memory: as complex, 150; as critical, 129; fear of losing, 126; handwriting increasing, 91; routines used for, 150–51; value of, 125
metacognition, 131; aspects of, 135; of children, 141, 150; as deep thinking, 134–36; desire influencing, 136; development of, 140, 178; encouraging of, 143, 149; practicing of, 144; questions encouraging, 135, 140; school presence of, 140–43; self-awareness from, 154; as success key, 134; teaching of, 133; understanding important for, 142, 150
Michener, James, 27
Milky Way, 78
mindfulness, 3, 85–86
mindset, 177, 182
Mitra, Sugata, 108, 127
Mona Lisa (da Vinci), 14, *15*
Moore, Gordon, 23
Muir, John, 12
multiple intelligences, 3
musical score, as linear, *13*

National Assessment Program-Literacy and Numeracy (NAPLAN), 30
National Geographic, 20

National Network of Partnership Schools, 3
National Research Council (NRC), 32
Netflix, 71
netiquette, 110
network: brain as, 61; disengaging from, 138; influence of, 63
No Child Left Behind, 30
note taking, 91
NRC. *See* National Research Council
numeracy, 4, 49

Obama, Barack (President), 76
obedience, 62, 67, 72
observing, 80
OMC. *See* Oxford Mindfulness Centre
Outliers (Gladwell), 54
Oxford Mindfulness Centre (OMC), 85

painting, 14
paraphrasing, 144, 171
parental controls, 111
parents: balance encouraged by, 87; boundaries enforced by, 113; as busy, 140; children assistance from, 46, 64, 186; engagement from, 1; limiting from, 98; safety taught by, 116; smart phones controlled by, 111
pausing, 144, 166, 171
Pavlov, Ivan, 32
Payne, Ruby, 39
persistence, 162–64
Pew Research Center, 100
phonemic awareness, 3
phonics-based learning, 3
Piaget, Jean, 35, 36
Picasso, Pablo, 15, *16*
Plato, 14, 17, 126
playing, 107, 108
political revolutions, 72
Pope, 77
pornography, 96, 112
praise: for children, 179; as problem, 178–80

prediction: of consequences, 147; as tool, 146
Prensky, Marc, 59, 104
printed language, 12, 16
printing press, 17
privacy settings: learning about, 115; for social media, 96, 115–16
probing, 144, 145, 166, 171
problem-solving: ability of, 5–6, 28–29; as collaborative, 5; critical thinking and, 45; as effective, 160; methods used for, 164; need for, 6; as opportunity, 143; as skill, 64; success in, 178; as talent, 132
punishments: for children, 33; emphasis on, 50. *See also* corporal punishment

questions: children benefitting from, 67; as complex, 149; deep thinking encouraged by, 128; interrogation compared to, 140; metacognition encouraged by, 135, 140; power of, 65–67, 148–49, 166, 171; process focus of, 149; social media prompting, 71; steps for asking, 145; as useful, 67; words for, 149–50

Ramachandran, V. M., 60
rational system of belief, 127
reading: comprehension of, 127; conversation replaced by, 69; as education focus, 17; misrepresentation of, 34; pace set by, 80; as private, 69
reasoning, 142
rebellion, 98–9
reflection: ability of, 160; as thinking tool, 135
Reigeluth, Charles, 35
Renaissance, 14, 27
rewards: for children, 33; emphasis on, 50; Internet as, 114
Robinson, Kenneth, 52, 153

rules: as boundaries, 110; for children, 72, 113; for Facebook groups, 169; understanding of, 151

The School of Athens, 14, *15*
schools: change reflected in, 73; community of, 3; dropping out of, 53–54; metacognition present in, 140–43; smart phones banned in, 114; subject content in schools, 124; teaching strategies in, 50; testing in, 52; view of, 49
Scientific Revolution, 18
search engines, 120–21. *See also* Google
Search for Extra Terrestrial Intelligence (SETI), 20
selectivity, 123
senses: awareness increased by, 86; learning of, 84; utilizing of, 92
Sensory Motor Stage, 36
sequencing, 136
SETI. *See* Search for Extra Terrestrial Intelligence
sexting, 97, 98
shape-shifting, 20–21
single view point, 14
skimming, 137
Skinner, B. F., 32, 179
sleep, benefit of, 128–29
smart phones: applications for, 109–10; appreciation decreased by, 101; awareness decreased by, 76, 83; banning of, 100, 114; manners for, 100; parents controlling, 111; rebellion encouraged by, 99; safe use of, 111
SMS messaging. *See* texting
Snopes, 120, 171
socialization, 77
social media: abusive use of, 117; applications for, 109; arguments on, 127, 181; awareness of, 23; as culture, 66; exploration through, 169; as fast, 103, 115;

implications of, 116–17; impulsivity encouraged by, 117; as informative, 110; interaction in, 81, 117; privacy settings for, 96, 115–16; questions prompted by, 71; safety on, 172; spread of, 114–18; vocabulary of, 167
Socrates, 29, 57, 125–26
specialization, as student requirement, 18–19
Spitzer, Manfred, 163
students: communication standards for, 6; creative thinking for, 50; encouraging of, 164; engagement of, 100; grades influencing, 180; mindset of, 182; specialization as requirement for, 18–19; twenty-first century skills for, 44
Summers, Mike, 46
surface thinking: binary thinking as, 93; digital world and, 81–82; generation of, 104
synthesizing, 151–52

tangible world: contact lost with, 78; digital world interactions with, 75–76, 79, 81; engagement with, 77, 84; Internet in, 76–77; safety in, 96; as sensory, 75; value of, 79–80
Taxonomy of Learning, 35
teachers: analogies utilized by, 27; challenges for, 167; change understood by, 24, 125; children assistance from, 46; curriculum for, 51; engagement from, 1; examples of, 55–57; filtering for, 3; as flexible, 51; judgments of, 167; lists utilized by, 66; processes utilized by, 143; tools provided by, 147; understanding taught by, 55
teaching: of analyzing, 123; beyond Google, 123; of handwriting, 89; learning compared to, 35; of metacognition, 133; of routines, 132;

schools strategies for, 50; words for thinking, 139
technology: assessment of, 136; in CCSS, 6, 96, 185; in classrooms, 96; as problem, 98, 105; rapid development of, 31; taking control of, 97; types of, 11; use of, 93
telemarketing, 171
television: benefit of, 69; children use of, 71; cinemas influenced by, 155; deep thinking from, 71; influence of, 163–64; as interactive, 70; interconnection through, 71; shared experience from, 70
The Tell-Tale Brain (Ramachandran), 60, 177
test scores, comparison instruments for, 29
texting, 82; engagement decreased by, 114; influence of, 154; problems with, 100; value of, 101. *See also* sexting
Thales, 29
theory of relativity, 13
thinking hats, 3
3D printing, 125
timing, 147–48
tools: analyzing as, 147; brain as important, 133; for children, 72, 127; for deep thinking, 134, 136, 138, 166; evaluation as, 152–153; pausing as, 166; prediction as, 146; reflection as, 135; teachers providing, 146; understanding of, 133; words as, 137–40
travel, 27
Twain, Mark, 121
twenty-first century: education tasks of, 127; skills for, 44; surviving in, 43–46
Twitter, 22, 61
typing: handwriting compared to, 92; as shouting, 111

UMMS. *See* University of Massachusetts Medical School
United States National Academy of Sciences, 44
University of Massachusetts Medical School (UMMS), 86
urban myths, 120

virtual world. *See* digital world
vocabulary, 139, 167
Vygotsky, Lev, 38

Wagner, Tony, 45
Walter, Marie-Therese, 15, *16*
Washington, George (President), 55
Wells, Gordon, 39
Wells, Orson, 120
Weschler, Arnold, 176
What the Internet is Doing to Our Brains: The Shallows (Carr), 154

Wikipedia, 22, 92, 122
women, education for, 29
words: children utilizing, 137; for questions, 149–50; spelling of, 168; for teaching thinking, 139; as tool, 137–40
world: brain and, 21–22; children view of, 51; complexities in, 28; as dynamic, 138; as fascinating, 83; shape-shifting in, 20–21. *See also* digital world; tangible world
World War I, 176
World Wide Web. *See* Internet
writing: CCSS standards for, 89, 123; characterization of, 12; curriculum for, 90; evolving of, 126. *See also* cursive writing; handwriting
The Wycliffe Bible, 17

YouTube, 71